MW01246058

DUKE
UNIVERSITY
LIBRARY

Treasure Room

GIFT OF

Mrs. W. L. Grissom

OUR OWN

SPELLING BOOK;

FOR THE USE OF

SCHOOLS AND FAMILIES.

BY

RICHARD STERLING, A. M.,

PRINCIPAL OF EDGEWORTH FEMALE SEMINARY,

AND

J. D. CAMPBELL, A. M.,

PROF. OF MATHEMATICS AND RHETORIC.

THIRD EDITION.

GREENSBORO, N. C.:

PUBLISHED BY STERLING, CAMPBELL & ALBRIGHT.

RICHMOND, VA.: W. HARGRAVE WHITE.

[illegible]

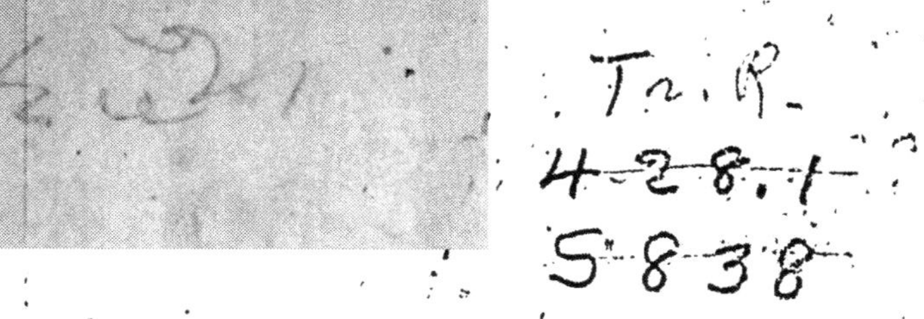

Entered according to Act of Congress,
in the year 1862, by
RICHARD STERLING & J. D. CAMPBELL,
In the Clerk's Office of the District Court of the Confederate States, for the District of Pamlico,
North Carolina.

PREFACE.

The design of this Spelling Book is to furnish an appropriate sequel to the Primer, of the elementary series, prepared by the authors of the present volume.

The Spelling-book now offered as an aid to elementary instruction, has been prepared to obviate, if possible, some of the difficulties that children must encounter in acquiring a correct knowledge of the Alphabet and the combinations of the sounds of letters in forming words.

Great care has been taken in the selection and classification of the words, and in the arrangement of the lessons, so as to lead the pupil gradually from easy to more difficult spelling.

In spelling and pronunciation we have followed, mainly, the authority of Dr. Worcester, who, in our judgement, approaches nearer the true English standard, and accords better with the usage of our best native authors in the Confederate States than any other lexicographer.

The classification of words according to the pronunciation of the accented syllable, long experience has taught us, is of great advantage to the pupil. Indeed system is an important aid in every department of education.

Since we learn the orthography of words chiefly that we may be able to write them correctly, it is a matter of surprise that more attention has not been paid to silent spelling by writing words from dictation. The most ex-

309375

peditious way of learning to spell is by the eye; and experienced teachers are well aware that many pupils will spell a word correctly, who if made to write it, will blunder.

We therefore earnestly recommend the constant use of the slate or blackboard as the easiest and most correct method of teaching orthography.

The reading lessons have been prepared with a two-fold object, first, to aid the pupil in learning to read, and second, to be used as dictation exercises for the slate or blackboard.

Another feature of this volume, to which we would ask the special attention of educators, is the exercises in analytical orthgraphy. We have furnished several lessons mearly as specimens The suggestions in these lessons, if applied throughout the entire book by the competent teacher, will furnish the pupil an amount of minute and accurate information he may never derive from any other source. Pupils should be carefully drilled in the analysis of one or more lessons every week, in which special attention should be given to the different sounds of each vowel.

THE ALPHABET.

Roman Letters.		*Italic Letters.*		*Script Letters.*			
A	a	*A*	*a*	*A*	*a*	*N*	*n*
B	b	*B*	*b*	*B*	*b*	*O*	*o*
C	c	*C*	*c*	*C*	*c*	*P*	*p*
D	d	*D*	*d*	*D*	*d*	*Q*	*q*
E	e	*E*	*e*	*E*	*e*	*R*	*r*
F	f	*F*	*f*	*F*	*f*	*S*	*s*
G	g	*G*	*g*	*G*	*g*	*T*	*t*
H	h	*H*	*h*	*H*	*h*	*U*	*u*
I	i	*I*	*i*	*I*	*i*	*V*	*v*
J	j	*J*	*j*	*J*	*j*	*W*	*w*
K	k	*K*	*k*	*K*	*k*	*X*	*x*
L	l	*L*	*l*	*L*	*l*	*Y*	*y*
M	m	*M*	*m*	*M*	*m*	*Z*	*z*
N	n	*N*	*n*				
O	o	*O*	*o*				
P	p	*P*	*p*				
Q	q	*Q*	*q*				
R	r	*R*	*r*				
S	s	*S*	*s*				
T	t	*T*	*t*				
U	u	*U*	*u*				
V	v	*V*	*v*				
W	w	*W*	*w*				
X	x	*X*	*x*				
Y	y	*Y*	*y*				
Z	z	*Z*	*z*				
			&			*J*	

Æ, Œ, æ, œ, fi, fl, ff, ffi, ffl

1, 2, 3, 4, 5, 6, 7, 8, 9, 10, 11, 12, 13, 14, 15.

309375

ANALYSIS OF THE ENGLISH ALPHABET.

The English Alphabet consists of twenty-six letters.

These are divided into vowels and consonants.

The vowels can be sounded without the aid of any other letter. They are *a*, *e*, *i*, *o*, *u*, and sometimes *w* and *y*.

The consonants cannot be sounded without the aid of a vowel. They are *b*, *c*, *d*, *f*, *g*, *h*, *j*, *k*, *l*, *m*, *n*, *p*, *q*, *r*, *s*, *t*, *v*, *x*, and *z*; and *w* and *y*, when they begin a word or syllable.

SOUNDS OF THE VOWELS.

A has five principal sounds; *E* has four; *I* has four; *O* has six; *U* has five; *Y* has three; and *W* one, as indicated in the following table:

A, as in fate[1], fat[2], far[3], fall[4], care[5].

E, as in mete[1], met[2], her[3], there[4].

I, as in pine[1], pin[2], sir[3], machine[4].

O, as in no[1], not[2], nor[3], move[4], done[5], wolf[6].

U, as in tube[1], tub[2], fur[3], full[4], rude[5].

Y, as in type[1], hymn[2], myrrh[3].

W has the sound of u long, as in *new*.

These vowels have also what is called the *slight* or *obscure* sound; and some of them, in words derived from foreign languages, retain the sounds peculiar to those languages.

A union of two vowels in one sound is called a *diphthong*; as, *oi* in oil; *oy* in boy; *ou* in round; *ow* in cow.

A union of three vowels in one sound is called a *triphthong*.

SOUNDS OF THE CONSONANTS.

B has but one sound, as in *bad*; after *m* and before *t*, it is silent, as in dum*b*, de*b*t.

C has two sounds, the hard like *k*, as in call; and the soft like *s*, as in cell.

It has the hard sound before *a*, *o*, *u*, *l*, *r*, and *t*, as in *case*, *cob*, *cure*, *clean*, *cry*, *strict*; the soft sound before *e*, *i*, and *y*, as in *cell*, *tacit*, *cypress*.

At the end of a word it is always hard, as in *music*, and before *k* it is silent, as in *back*.

D has one sound, as in day. At the end of a word after a silent *e*, it sometimes has the sound of *t*, as fixed, pronounced *fixt*.

F has one sound, as in *fat*; except in *of* it has the sound of *v*.

G has two sounds; it is hard before the letters, *a*, *u*, *l*, and *r*, and at the end of a word, as in *gate*, *go*, *gun*, *glad*, *grow*, *bag*, ; and generally soft before *e*, *i*, and *y*, as in *gem*, *giant*, *gypsum*. Before *m* and *n* it is silent, as in *g*naw, phle*g*m.

H is merely a breathing, as in *hate*. It is silent at the begining of many words; and generally after *g* and *r*; and at the end of a word, when preceded by a vowel.

K has the sound of *c* hard. Before *n* it is always silent, as in *k*nife.

L has one sound, as in *hill*. It is often silent.

M has one sound, as in *man*.

N has two sounds; the simple, as in *not;* and the nasal, as in *finger*, *sink*.

P has one sound, as in *pin*. Before *n*, *s*, and *t* at the begining of a word it is silent.

Q has but one sound. It is always followed by *u*, and has the sound of *k* or *kw*, as in *coquette*, *queen*.

R has two sounds, the rough, as in *run;* and the smooth, as in *arm*.

S has two principal sounds, the sharp, as in *hiss;* and the flat like *z*, as in *his*, *rise*. It has also the sound of *sh*, as in *sure*, and of *zh*, as in *measure*.

T has one principal sound, as in *not*. When followed by *ia*, *ie*, and *io*, it often combines with the *i*, and has the sound of *sh*, as in *partial*, *patient*, *nation*.

V has one sound, as in *vine*.

W, at the begining of a word or syllable, is a consonant, and is silent before *r*, as *write*, *bewray*.

X has three sounds, like *ks*, in *wax*, *gz* in *exalt*, and *z* in *Xerxes*.

Y, when a consonant, has one sound, as in *yet*.

Z has one principal sound, as in *zone*. It sometimes has the sound of *zh*, as in *azure*.

Ch has three sounds, like *tsh*, in *chain;* like *sh*, in *machine;* and like *k*, in *chord*.

Gh has three sounds, like *g*, in *ghost;* like *f*, in *cough;* and like *k*, in *hough*.

The letters *o u g h* have a variety of dissimilar sounds, as may be seen in the following stanza:

"'Tis not an easy task to show
How *o u g h* sounds; since, though
An Irish *lough* and English *slough*,
And *cough* and *hiccough*, all allow,
Differ as much as *though* and *through*,
There seems no reason why they do."

Ph generally has the sound of *f*, as in *physic*; in *stephen* it has the sound of *v*.

Th has two sounds, the hard or aspirate, as in *thin*; and the soft or flat, as in *this*.

Wh is sounded as if written *hw*, as in *when*, *whip*.

SYLLABLES AND WORDS.

A syllable is a letter, or union of letters, which can be pronounced by a single impulse of the voice; as, *a*, *bad*, *good*.

Words are made up of letters, or of syllables; as, *not*, *notion*. A word of *one* syllable is called a *monosyllable*; as *man*. A word of *two* syllables is called a *dissyllable*; as *manly*. A word of *three* syllables is called a *trisyllable*; as *manliness*.

Words of more than *three* syllables are called *polysyllables*; as, *luminary*, *incomprehensible*.

Accent is a stress of voice placed upon some one syllable more than the others.

Every word which is composed of more than one syllable, has one of its syllables accented. This accent is denoted by a mark over the accented syllable (′); as, mid′night, aban′don.

A primitive word is one which is not derived from any other word; as, *man*, *great*, *full*.

A derivative word is one which is formed from

some other word by adding something to it; as, *manly, greatness, folly.*

A simple word is one which is not composed of more than one word; as, *kind, man, stand, ink.*

A compound word is made up of two or more simple words; as, *man-kind, ink-stand.*

Spelling or orthography is expressing a word by its proper letters, in their regular order.

RULES FOR THE USE OF CAPITAL LETTERS.

1. Begin with a capital the first word of every sentence.

2. Begin with capitals all proper nouns, and titles of office, honor, and respect.

3. Begin with capitals all adjectives formed from proper nouns; as, *Roman, English.*

4. Begin with a capital the first word of every line of poetry.

5. Begin with capitals all appellations of the Deity, and the personal pronouns *he* and *thou*, when standing for His name.

6. Begin with a capital every noun, adjective and verb in the titles of books and headings of chapters.

7. The pronoun *I*, and the interjection *O*, must always be written with capitals.

2 3 4 5 6 1 2 3 4 5 1 2 3 1
not nor move done wolf–tube tub fur full rude–type hymn myrrh–new

LESSON 1.

Syllables and words of two letters.

1	1	1	1	1	1
Ba	be	bi	bo	bu	by
da	de	di	do	du	dy
fa	fe	fi	fo	fu	fy
ha	he	hi	ho	hu	hy
ja	je	ji	jo	ju	jy
ka	ke	ki	ko	ku	ky

1	1	2	2	2	1
Be	me	am	if	on	ho
by	my	as	in	ox	we
lo	no	at	is	or	[illegible]
go	so	an	it	up	do
he	ho	ax	of	us	to

LESSON 2.

Syllables of two letters.

1	1	1	1	1	1
La	le	li	lo	lu	ly
ma	me	mi	mo	mu	my
na	ne	ni	no	nu	ny
pa	pe	pi	po	pu	py
ra	re	ri	ro	ru	ry
sa	se	si	so	su	sy

2	2	2	2	2
Ab	eb	ib	ob	ub
ac	ec	ic	oc	uc
ad	ed	id	od	ud
[illegible]	ef	if	of	uf
[illegible]	eg	ig	og	ug

LESSON 3.

Syllables of two letters.

2	2	2	2	2
Ak	ek	ik	ok	uk
al	el	il	ol	ul
am	em	im	om	um
an	en	in	on	un
ap	ep	ip	op	up
as	es	is	os	us

Is he in? He is in. Is he in it? He is in it. I am by it. It is by me. Go to it. He is on it. Go up on it. I am up on it.

Is it an ox? It is an ox. Is he on an ox? He is on an ox. Is it my ox? It is my ox.

LESSON 4.

Syllables of three letters.

1	1	1	1	1	1
Bla	ble	bli	blo	blu	[illegible]
fla	fle	fli	flo	flu	[illegible]
gla	gle	gli	glo	glu	[illegible]
pla	ple	pli	plo	plu	[illegible]
sla	sle	sli	slo	slu	[illegible]

1	1	1	1	1	1
Bra	bre	bri	bro	bru	[illegible]
cra	cre	cri	cro	cru	[illegible]
dra	dre	dri	dro	dru	[illegible]
fra	fre	fri	fro	fru	[illegible]
gra	gre	gri	gro	gru	[illegible]
pra	pre	pri	pro	pru	[illegible]

2	3	4	5	6	1	2	3	4	5	1	2	3	1
not	nor	move	done	wolf–	tube	tub	fur	full	rude–	type	hymn	myrrh–	new

LESSON 5.

Words of three letters.

2	2	2	2	2	2	2
Bad	nag	cap	mat	bed	pen	bin
gad	tag	gap	pat	fed	ten	din
had	wag	lap	rat	led	wen	fin
lad	rag	map	sat	wed	bet	gin
mad	lag	nap	ham	beg	get	pin
pad	ban	nab	jam	keg	jet	sin
sad	can	sap	ram	leg	let	tin
bag	fan	tap	yam	peg	met	win
cab	man	bat	dam	den	net	vet
fag	pan	cat	lax	fen	pet	vat
gag	ran	fat	tax	hen	set	not
hag	tan	hat	wax	men	wet	jot

LESSON 6.

Words of three letters.

2	2	2	2	2	2	3
Dip	pit	fob	fop	bug	but	bar
hip	sit	job	hop	hug	cut	car
lip	fit	mob	lop	mug	hut	far
nip	wit	cob	top	rug	nut	jar
pip	fix	nod	cot	gum	dug	mar
rip	mix	pod	dot	hum	fig	tar
sip	six	rod	got	rum	rig	her
tip	vex	bog	hot	sum	wig	fir
bit	sex	dog	lot	fun	cub	sir
[illegible]	box	fog	not	gun	hub	bur
nit	pox	log	rot	sun	rub	fur

1 2 3 4 5 1 2 3 4 1 2 3 4 1
fate fat far fall care—mete met her there—pine pin sir machine—no

LESSON 7.

Words of three letters.

1	1	1	1	1	2
Bay	bee	dew	aid	ace	act
day	fee	few	aim	age	add
gay	lee	hew	ail	ale	aft
hay	see	jew	ait	ape	and
jay	doe	new	ear	ate	apt
lay	hoe	pew	eel	ake	ask
may	roe	mew	oak	ice	ebb
nay	toe	cue	oar	ode	egg
pay	die	due	oat	ore	elk
ray	lie	hue	oad	oke	ell
say	pie	rue	oaf	ope	elm
way	tie	sue	eat	use	end

LESSON 8.

Words of three letters.

2	2	2	2	2	4
Lag	web	rap	his	him	jaw
wag	mop	cup	cog	cub	law
cob	sod	sup	jug	pig	maw
sob	hid	yet	web	bud	saw
hem	bid	gem	tug	mud	taw
ban	big	kin	dim	tan	raw

It is the lot of all men to die. You are to die. My son, go not in the way of bad men. God can see us, and all we do. You can not see God; but he can see you and me. His [illegible] us all the Day. All men sin. But Go[illegible] sin, or do a bad act.

LESSON 9.

Words of four letters.

1	1	1	1	1	1
Bake	pave	dace	sage	bile	code
cake	rave	face	wage	file	mode
lake	save	lace	date	mile	none
make	wave	mace	hate	pile	cone
rake	made	pace	late	hide	hope
sake	fade	race	mate	ride	mope
take	jade	cape	pate	side	pope
wake	wade	tape	sate	tide	rope
cave	came	cage	game	dine	mule
gave	dame	gage	name	line	cure
lave	fame	page	same	nine	lure
nave	lame	rage	tame	pine	pure

LESSON 10.

Words of four letters.

1	1	1	1	1	1
Bite	bide	fine	base	tole	hose
rite	jibe	kine	bane	tone	nose
mite	dive	mine	mane	zone	rose
site	five	vine	gaze	lope	cove
kite	hive	wine	haze	cope	rove
[illegible]	hire	ripe	maze	core	wove
[illegible]	dire	wipe	bole	gore	hove
[illegible]	mire	type	dole	more	cube
[illegible]	fire	cite	hole	sore	tube
[illegible]	sire	sine	mole	tore	tune
[illegible]	tire	pyre	pole	wore	June
[illegible]	wire	lyre	sole	bore	duke

LESSON 11.

Words of four letters.

2	2	2	2	2	2
Crab	brag	cram	chap	chip	grip
drab	crag	dram	flap	ship	snip
blab	drag	clam	slip	whip	spit
slab	flag	slam	brat	flip	grit
stab	snag	bran	plat	slip	crib
shot	stag	clan	slat	drip	glib
spot	club	plod	bed	chin	brad
blot	drub	shod	fled	grin	shad
plot	drug	trod	sled	spin	clad
grot	slug	clog	sped	skim	plan
trot	snug	flog	whet	slim	scan
prop	shut	frog	when	brim	span

LESSON 12.

Words of four letters.

2	2	2	2	2	
Camp	best	bell	kick	cull	bump
damp	lest	cell	lick	dull	dump
lamp	rest	dell	neck	gull	hump
ramp	test	fell	pick	hull	lump
samp	vest	tell	sick	mull	pump
vamp	west	well	tick	null	rump
cash	bent	bill	dock	duck	[illegible]
dash	cent	fill	hock	luck	mush
gash	dent	hill	lock	muck	bush
lash	lent	kill	nock	puck	rush
rash	vent	mill	rock	suck	bull
sash	went	sill	sock	tuck	[illegible]

2 3 4 5 6 1 2 3 4 5 1 2 3 1
not nor move done wolf—tube tub fur full rude—type hymn myrrh—new

LESSON 13.

Words of four letters.

2	2	2	2	2	2
Clap	bred	clip	chop	drub	grin
snap	dred	skip	drop	snub	swim
flap	tred	skin	crop	stub	smit
flat	sned	slit	shop	drum	whit
flux	shed	flit	slop	grum	snib
glad	sted	snip	stop	plum	prig
grab	stem	trip	grog	scum	sham
scab	fret	prim	clot	scud	swam
chat	tret	trim	from	chum	plug
tram	snet	whim	scot	slum	flux
trap	glen	twin	clod	stun	swop
slap	step	shin	snob	glum	trig

LESSON 14.

Words of four letters.

		2	2	2	2
[illegible]	band	bond	hilt	gift	help
[illegible]	hand	fond	link	lift	left
[illegible]	land	pond	mink	sift	felt
[illegible]	sand	fund	pink	[illegible]	melt
[illegible]	[illegible]	much	sink	[illegible]	pelt
[illegible]	lend	such	wink	[illegible]	belt
[illegible]	[illegible]	dusk	limp	[illegible]	welt
[illegible]	send	husk	lint	risk	wept
	[illegible]	[illegible]	dint	[illegible]	[illegible]
[illegible]	[illegible]	[illegible]	mint	[illegible]	[illegible]
	wend	milk	[illegible]	[illegible]	[illegible]
	[illegible]	silk	hint	[illegible]	[illegible]

1 2 3 4 5 1 2 3 4 1 2 3 4 1
fate fat far fall care—mete met her there—pine pin sir machine—n o

LESSON 15.

THE RIDE.

Come now, let us go and take a ride.

Do not fear, we will not ride fast.

So put on your coat, and make it fast with the belt.

The girl puts on her belt, she will not fear.

The boy has a whip in his hand and a cap on his head.

He can ride fast, but he will not, for he told the girl so.

They will ride out, and see the men at work in the lot.

The air is fine, and they will have a nice ride.

LESSON 16.

Words of four letters.

3	3	3	3	3	3
Cart	bask	born	jerk	curd	bard
dart	cask	corn	hurt	curb	card
hart	mask	fork	turf	surf	hard
mart	task	form	lurk	bird	lard
part	hasp	lord	burn	gird	barn
tart	rasp	cord	turn	firm	kern
bark	bass	sort	dirk	term	[illegible]
dark	lass	tort	kirk	verd	[illegible]
hark	pass	dirt	curl	[illegible]	fern
lark	mass	girl	furl	[illegible]	[illegible]
mark	haft	surd	hurl	[illegible]	[illegible]
park	raft	purr	mirk	girl	[illegible]

2	3	4	5	6	1	2	3	4	5	1	2	3	1
not	nor	move	done	wolf–	tube	tub	fur	full	rude–	type	hymn	myrrh–	new

LESSON 17.

Words of four letters, containing a double vowel.

1	1	1	6	4	4
Feel	deem	lees	book	cool	moon
keel	seem	beer	cook	coop	loom
reel	teem	deer	foot	boot	soon
keep	leek	jeer	good	food	boon
weep	week	bees	hood	doom	loon
deed	heel	beet	hook	fool	pool
feed	peel	feet	nook	root	tool
heed	keen	peep	look	moon	hoot
weed	seen	reef	took	boom	moor
meek	leer	seed	wood	room	poor
seek	peer	weep	wool	rood	moor
reek	seer	veer	hoop	roof	woof

LESSON 18.

Words of four letters.

4	4	3	2	2	1
Fall	halt	farm	cost	fast	bind
[illegible]	salt	harm	fuss	mast	find
ball	wasp	yard	moss	waft	hind
gall	wand	yarn	bung	past	kind
hall	swan	garb	sung	vast	mind
mall	wart	harp	loll	last	bolt
pall	warp	stir	pulp	tost	colt
[illegible]	warm	verb	desk	lest	dolt
wall	warn	arch	lost	test	jolt
	malt	born	long	pest	told
	[illegible]	fern	lens	vest	torn
	wast	herd	lisp	west	worn

1 2 3 4 5 1 2 3 4 1 2 3 4 1
fate fat far fall care—mete met her there—pine pin sir machine—no

LESSON 19.

Words of five letters.

1	1	1	1	
Blame	brave	chase	bride	drove
flame	crave	brace	chide	grove
shame	grave	grace	bribe	stove
shape	shave	place	tribe	stone
crape	slave	glaze	glide	store
grape	stave	stage	slide	snore
blade	shake	plate	shine	score
glade	snake	state	swine	scope
grade	stake	slate	smite	globe
shade	spake	crate	snipe	spoke
spade	flake	frame	brine	smoke
trade	brake	crane	twine	slope

LESSON 20.

ANALYSIS.

What is the sound of *a* in the word *blame*?

It has the long sound as in *fate*.

Is *a* a vowel or a consonant, and why?

It is a vowel, because it can be sounded without the aid of any other letter.

Can you name the vowels?

They are *a*, *e*, *i*, *o*, *u* and sometimes *w* and *y*.

What are the other letters called?

They are called consonants.

What is a consonant?

A consonant is a letter that cannot be sounded without the aid of a vowel.

Note.—Let the teacher ask similar questions on other words.

2	3	5	5	6	1	2	3	4	5	1	2	3	1
not	nor	move	done	wolf	tube	tub	fur	full	rude	type	hymn	myrrh	new

LESSON 21.

Words of five letters.

2	2	2	2	2
Blank	crack	blest	bring	crock
flank	track	chest	cling	frock
plank	stack	blend	fling	block
crank	slack	spend	swing	clock
drank	frank	spent	brink	shock
prank	clank	bless	drink	stock
cramp	speck	chess	slink	clung
stamp	smell	dress	brick	flung
grand	spell	tress	stick	stung
brand	shell	crest	trick	slung
gland	smelt	fresh	click	blush
stand	spelt	cress	crick	crush

LESSON 22.

Words of two syllables, accented on the first.

1	1	1	1	1
Ba'by	di'al	he'ro	[illegible]	[illegible]
la dy	[illegible]	ve to	[illegible]	[illegible]
[illegible]	[illegible]	ze ro	[illegible]	ru by
[illegible]	[illegible]	re al	so [illegible]	[illegible]
[illegible]	[illegible]	bo ny	[illegible]	[illegible]
[illegible]	ri ot	co ny	[illegible]	
[illegible]	ri al	[illegible]	[illegible]	
[illegible]	vi al	[illegible]	[illegible]	
wa ry	[illegible]	[illegible]	du [illegible]	
[illegible]	[illegible]	[illegible]	[illegible]	
[illegible]	[illegible]	[illegible]	[illegible]	
[illegible]	[illegible]	[illegible]	[illegible]	

1 2 3 4 5 1 2 3 4 1 2 3 4 1
fate fat far fall care—mete met her there—pine pin sir machine—no

LESSON 23.

Words of two syllables, accented on the first.

1	1	1	1	1
Ba'ker	le'gal	fi'nal	lo'cal	cu'bit
fa tal	re gal	ri val	fo cal	hu mid
na tal	pe nal	vi tal	vo cal	tu mid
pa pal	ve nal	vi per	po lar	tu lip
ta per	ce dar	ti ler	so lar	tu tor
ca per	ne gro	ci der	mo lar	tu mor
pa per	fe ver	di ver	do nor	lu rid
pa gan	le ver	ri pen	so ber	hu man
Sa tan	la bor	mi ser	to per	ru mor
ma ker	fa vor	si lex	to tal	mu sic
ta ker	va por	pi lot	po ker	ma son
ra cer	ra zor	ti ger	to ken	wa ger

LESSON 24.

Words of two syllables, accented on the first.

2	2	2	2	2
[illegible]	car'ry	ber'ry	civ'il	col'ic
[illegible]	mar ry	fer ry	dit ty	dor ic
[illegible]	[illegible] ry	mer ry	gid dy	ton ic
[illegible]	tar ry	mer it	fil ly	top ic
[illegible]	ral ly	jel ly	sil ly	mot to
[illegible]	sal ly	jet ty	liv id	fol ly
[illegible]	tal ly	pen ny	lim it	jol ly
[illegible]	hab it	lep er	lin en	mud dy
[illegible]	nap py	tep id	liv er	rud dy
[illegible]	rap id	nev er	riv er	pup py
[illegible]	can to	sev er	riv et	put ty
[illegible]	can dy	bev el	piv ot	gul ly

LESSON 25.

ANALYSIS.

On which syllable is the accent in *shady?*
The first

What is the vowel sound in the accented syllable? The long sound

What is the vowel sound in the unaccented syllable? The short sound of *y*.

What figure marks the long vowel sound?
The figure 1.

What figure marks the short vowel sound?
The figure 2.

How many sounds has *a*?
A has five sounds marked 1, 2, 3, 4, 5.
How many has each of the other vowels?

LESSON 26.

THE GOOD BOY.

When a good boy comes into the house, he always takes off his hat or cap, and hangs it on a nail, or puts it away in its proper place.

When he wishes to go out, he knows where to find his hat, for he never leaves it on the floor or chairs, or where it may be lost.

[illegible] a place for everything, and [illegible] [illegible] in its place, so that he could [illegible] [illegible], even in the dark.

[illegible] books and his clothes are [illegible] [illegible]. No spots of ink are ever [illegible]

1 2 3 4 5 1 2 3 4 1 2 3 4 1
fate fat far fall care—mete met her there—pine pin sir machine—no

LESSON 27.

Words of five letters.

2	3	3	4	4
Blast	shark	chirp	bloom	brood
clasp	spark	flirt	broom	droop
grasp	stark	shirt	groom	scoop
flask	sharp	skirt	gloom	swoon
shaft	smart	smirk	proof	swoop
craft	start	third	troop	scald
graft	clerk	whirl	stoop	small
chaff	sperm	twirl	stool	stall
staff	stern	spirt	spool	sward
brass	chart	churn	spoon	swarm
class	charm	spurn	shoot	dwarf
grass	snarl	churl	sloop	wharf

LESSON 28.

Words of five letters.

1	2	2	3	4
Baste	batch	mince	carve	cause
haste	catch	since	farce	sauce
paste	hatch	wince	parse	fault
taste	latch	ditch	barge	[illegible]
waste	match	hitch	large	waltz
range	patch	pitch	merge	booth
mange	bench	copse	burst	goose
[illegible]	dense	dodge	curst	moose
	fence	lodge	durst	noose
	pence	notch	purge	loose
	hence	dunce	surge	[illegible]
	sense	mumps	curve	[illegible]

2 3 4 5 6 1 2 3 4 5 1 2 3 1
not nor move done wolf—tube tub fur full rude—type hymn myrrh—new

LESSON 29.

Words of one syllable, in which the second vowel is silent.

1	1	1	1	1
Sea	deal	cream	paid	train
pea	meal	dream	staid	grain
tea	seal	gleam	fail	chain
plea	veal	steam	jail	drain
flea	near	cheat	nail	stain
beam	dear	treat	pail	slain
meal	heat	cheap	braid	faint
read	neat	peach	flail	paint
ream	seat	teach	frail	saint
seam	heap	reach	snail	taint
year	leap	speak	quail	claim
gear	east	feast	trail	trait

LESSON 30.

Words of one syllable, in which the second vowel is silent.

1	2	1	1	1
Oak	dead	bloat	baize	crow
coal	head	gloat	raise	snow
foal	bread	float	maize	grow
loam	dread	shoal	seize	stow
roam	lead	croak	sheaf	glow
foam	read	boast	leaf	show
load	stead	board	clay	bowl
toad	tread	coach	pray	sown
boat	sweat	oath	bray	flown
goat	death	toast	dray	grown
soap	deaf	coax	sway	blown
soak	meant	hoax	spray	flow

LESSON 31.

Words of one syllable, in which the first vowel is silent.

1	1	1	1	5
Brief	great	brew	jew	bear
chief	shield	crew	dew	pear
grief	fierce	drew	mew	tear
thief	pierce	flew	new	wear
fiend	tierce	grew	pew	swear
field	grieve	hew	yew	2
wield	priest	chew	clew	built
yield	shriek	screw	spew	build
niece	fief	shew	few	guilt
piece	pier	strew	view	guild
liege	tier	stew	lieu	guess
siege	bier	blew	feud	guest

LESSON 32.

Words containing *oi*, *oy*, and *ow*.

oi	oy	ou	ou	ow
Oil	boy	out	bound	cow
boil	coy	pout	found	howl
coil	joy	rout	hound	prowl
foil	toy	shout	mound	scowl
soil	cloy	spout	pound	growl
toil	troy	stout	round	down
broil	hoy	trout	sound	clown
spoil	moy	gout	wound	town
coin	moyle	snout	count	brown
join	boyn	clout	mount	frown
groin	foy	flour	fount	crown
joint	soy	sour	bounce	drown

2	3	4	5	6	1	2	3	4	5	1	2	3	1
not	nor	move	done	wolf-	tube	tub	fur	fell	rude-	type	hymn	myrrh-	new

LESSON 33.

Words of two syllables, accented on the first.

1	1	2	2
Dan′ger	bro′ker	ban′ter	bet′ter
man ger	clo ver	ham mer	fet ter
qua ker	dro ver	ban ner	let ter
qua ver	gro cer	ham per	fes ter
dra per	fro zen	man ner	pes ter
fla vor	bro ken	pal lid	pep per
tre mor	flo ral	pan try	ren der
spi der	stu pid	rab bit	gen der
cli ent	stu por	ban ish	rec tor
spi ral	blu ish	can cer	but ter
cli max	flu ent	bat ter	gut ter
cri sis	plu ral	mat ter	mut ter

LESSON 34.

Words of two syllables, accented on the first.

2	2	3	2
Bib′ber	col′lar	bar′ber	sim′per
bit ter	dol lar	bar ter	sis ter
dif fer	doc tor	car pet	win ter
din ner	cop per	gar ter	vic tor
fit ter	fod der	mar tin	lic tor
lit ter	pot ter	mar tyr	tin dor
tin ner	fos ter	her mit	ten der
sin ner	gos pel	ser mon	dex ter
gin ger	pon der	ver min	fen der
lim ber	fot ter	mur der	suf fer
sil ver	yon der	mur mur	sup per
sim mer	bon net	tur nip	rud der

LESSON 35.

Words of two syllables, accented on the first.

1	1	2	2
Cham′ber	molt′en	stam′mer	slen′der
hast en	dole ful	can ter	shel ter
shak en	fore man	plat ter	meth od
trad er	port ly	plant er	nest ling
past ry	fore most	plan et	clev er
hast y	port al	van ish	frit ter
like ly	port er	plas tic	glit ter
like wise	duke dom	rack et	glim mer
sli my	tune ful	land ing	shiv er
dri ver	cure less	chap ter	quiv er
hire ling	pure ly	bank er	shut ter
Fri day	use ful	bran dy	stut ter

LESSON 36.

Words of two syllables, accented on the first.

2	2	2	4
Ab′bot	clam′or	check′er	hal′ter
at om	lan tern	splen did	fal ter
ash es	mat ron	lev el	pal try
cam let	gant let	ves per	wan der
cap tor	haz ard	west ern	wan ton
car rot	pack et	cit y	quar rel
cav il	par rot	din gy	quar ry
chap let	mas tic	diz zy	pal sy
chat tel	rag ged	fin ish	bal sam
gal lon	ran dom	gim let	pal ter
gal lop	pat tern	tim id	al tar
mat ter	val id	spir it	al ways

2 3 4 5 6 1 2 3 4 5 1 2 3 1
not nor move done wolf tube tub far fall rude–type hymn myrrh–new

LESSON 37.

A LITTLE GIRL'S LETTER.

1. I will show you a little girl's letter to her friend at school. The name of the little girl is Mary. She wrote the letter from a house near the sea-side, where she will stay for a short time with her aunt.

2. Here is the letter: "I hope you are quite well. We are all quite well. There is a large, white cat here; its eyes are red, or, I should say, pink. It wears a black band round its neck, with a small bell tied to it.

3. "When she walks, the bell rings. I like to hear the sound of this bell. We know where the cat is; for, when she moves, the bell rings.

4. "Now, you will like to hear why the cat wears the bell. She goes into the woods near the house, where there are birds; the birds can hear the bell, and can take care that the cat does not catch them.

5. "There is a tame dove here, too, which comes out of its cage, and flies through the rooms. No doubt, you think that the cat would catch the dove? No, they are good friends; such good friends, that the dove will sit on the cat's head, and the cat does not hurt it.

6. "I shall try to tame our bird and cat, that they may be as good friends as this cat and dove are. And now, good-by, till I write again."

LESSON 38.

Words of two syllables, accented on the second.

1	1	2	3
A wake′	e late′	a bash′	a far′
a woke	e vade	a bet	a larm
a rise	e rase	a las	a part
a rose	e lope	a dopt	a lert
a bide	e voke	a bed	a ver
a bode	e lide	a mend	a verse
a lone	e duce	a mid	a vert
a shore	a pace	e lect	e merge
a tone	a muse	e rect	a merce
a like	a cute	e ject	a bort
a live	u nite	e vent	a dorn
a bate	o blige	e vince	a jar

LESSON 39.

Words of two syllables, accented on the second.

1	1	1	1
Be came′	ac cede′	be hind′	in voke′
be have	ad here	re cite	re voke
de base	com plete	po lite	ca jole
be take	con cede	be side	com pose
se date	con vene	be tide	en robe
di late	im pede	ig nite	ex plode
for sake	re cede	re vile	de pose
ef face	re plete	de ny	ex pose
em pale	re verse	re ply	de mure
es tate	se crete	de fy	im mure
de bate	se rene	Ju ly	re fute
in vade	se vere	de cry	re pute

2 3 4 5 6 1 2 3 4 5 1 2 3 1
not nor move done wolf–tube tub fur full rude–type hymn myrrh–new

LESSON 40.

Words of one syllable.

2	2	3	5	1
Badge	lodge	dirge	done	scrape
fadge	podge	merge	front	stake
edge	budge	serge	wont	flake
hedge	judge	verge	dove	chafe
ledge	grudge	verse	love	strange
pledge	hinge	terse	glove	graze
fledge	cringe	urge	shove	blaze
sledge	fringe	surd	come	chime
wedge	singe	scorn	none	price
ridge	twinge	snort	monk	slice
bridge	plunge	gorge	month	spice
midge	lunge	storm	sponge	nice

LESSGN 41.

Words of one syllable, ending in *ch* soft.

2	2	2	2	1
French	inch	batch	pitch	beech
bench	finch	catch	hitch	le*a*ch
blench	pinch	hatch	witch	te*a*ch
drench	winch	latch	flitch	pre*a*ch
belch	flinch	match	stitch	pe*a*ch
tench	clinch	patch	twitch	ble*a*ch
trench	filch	snatch	notch	re*a*ch
quench	pilch	scratch	scotch	speech
wench	bunch	fetch	blotch	porch
clench	hunch	ketch	crotch	po*a*ch
stench	lunch	retch	crutch	ro*a*ch
which	munch	stretch	hutch	co*a*ch

LESSON 42.

Words in which *th* has the hard or aspirate sound.

2	2	1	2	1
Thin	thank	thane	bath	both
think	thatch	theme	lath	lo*a*th
thing	thrash	thrive	path	quoth
thrift	throb	thrice	hath	gro*w*th
thrill	thong	throw	broth	forth
thick	throng	throne	cloth	fo*u*rth
thre*a*d	thug	thro*a*t	froth	sloth
theft	thre*a*t	throve	moth	o*a*th
thrust	thill	thole	filth	truth
thump	thilk	thre*w*	frith	youth
thrush	thack	three	width	she*a*th
thrum	third	thro*e*	smith	teeth

LESSON 43.

Words of two syllables, accented on the second.

1	1	2	5
De cide′	con fide′	ap ply′	con clude′
de file	con fine	im ply	pre clude
de fine	con spire	com ply	se clude
de ride	ex pire	es py	al lude
de sire	re spire	sup ply	de lude
di vide	re tire	re ly	pol lude
di vine	re quire	de duce	pro trude
ar rive	ac quire	com mute	in trude
as cribe	re cline	ma ture	in clude
as pire	re fine	pro cure	con sume
at tire	re pine	en dure	as sume
bap tize	com bine	al ly	sa lute

2	3	4	5	6	1	2	3	4	5	1	2	3	1
not	nor	move	done	wolf–	tube	tub	fur	full	rude–	type	hymn	myrrh–	new

LESSON 44.

Words of two syllables, accented on the second.

2	2	2	2
Ca nal′	be deck′	re ject′	as sist′
cra vat	be held	re sent	en list
de camp	be quest	re quest	en rich
de cant	de fect	re spect	com mit
de tract	de ject	ef fect	dis til
pro tract	de test	ex tend	ful fil
re cant	pre tend	ex tent	ad mit
re fract	pre vent	in tend	ad dict
re lax	pro tect	in tent	at tact
re tract	re flect	in ject	dis patch
se dan	re fresh	neg lect	dis tract
at tract	re lent	se lect	ex pand

LESSON 45.

Words of two syllables, accented on the second.

2	2	1	2
Pro ject′	sup plant′	pro ceed′	pre fer′
sub ject	im plant	gen teel	per vert
con nect	fer ment	set tee	de fer
col lect	dis sent	suc ceed	sub vert
sus pect	re pent	con cise	ex pert
cor rect	pre fix	per spire	in vert
pre dict	per plex	sub lime	in ter
con flict	con sult	sur vive	in fer
dis tinct	cor rupt	com port	con cur
ex tinct	con tend	con dole	dis turb
con duct	con fess	con sole	ab surd
con struct	per haps	con trol	de mur

LESSON 46.

Words of two syllables, accented on the first, and in which the final *e* is silent.

1	2	2	2
Ca′ble	am′ble	ket′tle	bot′tle
fa ble	am ple	net tle	cob ble
ga ble	ap ple	peb ble	fon dle
sa ble	bab ble	set tle	hob ble
ta ble	baf fle	brit tle	bub ble
sta ble	bat tle	dim ple	bun dle
la dle	cat tle	fid dle	crum ble
ma ple	daz zle	kin dle	muf fle
sta ple	grap ple	lit tle	muz zle
bri dle	han dle	pim ple	pud dle
no ble	man tle	rid dle	puz zle

LESSON 47.

Words of two syllables, in which the final *e* is silent.

1	2	2	3
Bi′ble	can′dle	nim′ble	mar′ble
ti tle	dan dle	tip ple	gar ble
tri fle	ram ble	tit tle	gar gle
i dle	sad dle	tin gle	spar kle
ri fle	raf fle	tin kle	star tle
sti fle	prat tle	mid dle	cir cle
cra dle	tat tle	fic kle	gir dle
la ble	sam ple	pic kle	cur dle
bee tle	tram ple	sim ple	hur dle
fee ble	tem ple	min gle	pur dle
bu gle	trem ble	thim ble	tur tle
scru ple	gen tle	whit tle	myr tle

LESSON 48.

Words of two syllables, accented on the second.

2	2	2	1
Be hest′	ex pel′	sub mit′	ac cuse′
be set	im pel	in flict	ad duce
ca det	ap pend	in struct	re buke
de pend	im pend	in duct	re duce
pro pel	fo ment	re sult	se cure
re pel	di rect	in sult	com mune
at tend	ex pect	con sent	com pute
an nex	be gin	la ment	con fute
com mend	de sist	dis sent	im pute
com pel	re mit	at test	in duce
dis pel	re sist	trans act	dis pute

LESSON 49.

Words in which *ti*, *si* and *ci* are pronounced like *sh*.

1	2	2	2
Na′tion	ac′tion	op′tion	cap′tious
sta tion	fac tion	unc tion	fac tious
mo tion	frac tion	junc tion	frac tious
no tion	trac tion	func tion	vi cious
lo tion	cap tion	suc tion	lus cious
po tion	sanction	man sion	pre cious
por tion	men tion	pas sion	spe cial
pa tient	sec tion	pen sion	3
quo tient	lec tion	ten sion	ver sion
gra cious	dic tion	ses sion	mer sion
spa cious	fic tion	mis sion	tor tion
spe cious	fric tion	ces sion	par tial

1 2 3 4 5 1 2 3 4 1 2 3 4 1
fate fat far fall care—mete met her there—pine pin sir machine—no

LESSON 50.

Words of three syllables, accented on the first.

	2	2	
No′ti fy	san′i ty	in′di go	pun′gen cy
pu ri ty	van i ty	in fa my	cus to dy
pi ra cy	par i ty	in ju ry	sol ven cy
no ta ry	lax i ty	en mi ty	in dus try
ro ta ry	len i ty	en er gy	con tra ry
vo ta ry	lev i ty	en e my	des per ate
pu ri ty	ver i ty	bot a ny	bib li cal
mu ti ny	cav i ty	fam i ly	an nu al
nu di ty	com i ty	par o dy	cop per as
cu ra cy	pol i ty	pen u ry	sup pli ant
po et ry	dim i ty	rem e dy	lux u ry
po e sy	dep u ty	col o ny	cod i cil

LESSON 51.

Words of three syllables, accented on the first.

1	2	2	3
Ra′di us	bal′co ny	her′ald ry	fer′ven cy
ra pi er	fac ul ty	big ot ry	fer til ize
la bi al	bar ri er	dig ni ty	ser mon ize
me ni al	gal ax y	his to ry	her mit age
jo vi al	den si ty	pil lo ry	tur pen tine
mu tu al	des ti ny	pen al ty	par son age
pe ri od	cen tu ry	nov el ty	par ti cle
glo ri fy	gen er al	nul li ty	har mo ny
stu pe fy	ten den cy	dig ni fy	har bin ger
flu en cy	ped ant ry	jus ti fy	mar tin gale
bri er y	ped es tal	nul li fy	mar tyr dom
ple na ry	her e sy	am pli fy	mer cu ry

2 3 4 5 6 1 2 3 4 5 1 2 3 1
not nor move done wolf–tube tub fur full rude–type hymn myrrh–new

LESSON 52.

ANALYSIS.

Where is the accent in *glorify?* On the first syllable.

How is it marked? It is marked with (′), called the accent mark.

What sound has the vowel in the accented syllable? It has the long sound, as in *no.*

How many sounds has *o?* It has six sounds.

Give the sound of *o* in *no, not, nor, move, done, wolf.*

What is *g?* It is a consonant.

How many sounds has *g?* It has two.

Which sound has it in *glorify?* The hard.

Before what letters is it always hard? Before *a, o, u, l,* and *r.*

Before what letters is it generally soft? Before *e, i,* and *y.*

Under what other circumstances is it always hard? At the end of a word, and at the end of a syllable, when the next syllable begins with a consonant.

How many syllables are there in *glorify?* Three.

What are words of three syllables called? Trisyllables.

What are words of two syllables called? Dissyllables.

What are words of more that three syllables called? Pollysyllables.

1 2 3 4 5 1 2 3 4 1 2 3 4 1
fate fat far fall care—mete met her there—pine pin sir machine—no

LESSON 53.

Words of three syllables, accented on the second.

1	1	2	3
Ar ma′da	ar ri′val	im pan′el	in fer′nal
ca na ry	re vi val	ap par el	ma ter nal
po ta to	de ni al	pi as ter	in ter nal
oc ta vo	re ci tal	pi las ter	pa ter nal
po ma tum	re pri sal	ro man cer	e ter nal
a wa ken	pro vi so	u ten sil	hi ber nal
ad ja cent	ho ri zon	in tend ant	noc tur nal
tor na do	re qui tal	de fend ant	di ur nal
vol ca no	in qui ry	as sev er	un cer tain
i de al	com pli ant	de liv er	con cur rent
co e val	tor pe do	e lix ir	in for mal
ad he rent	in he rent	un civ il	im por tant

LESSON 54.

Words of three syllables, accented on the second.

2	2	1	2
Me men′to	dis as′ter	en dan′ger	in clem′ent
mu lat to	un fast en	ver ba tim	pa rent al
de vel op	to bac co	ad ja cent	pre cep tor
en vel op	com pos ite	pri me val	pro mul gate
pa thet ic	a pos tate	pro ced ure	en cum ber
cos met ic	de pos it	ca the dral	en sam ple
do mes tic	pro con sul	com pos ure	ex am ple
sur ren der	co los sal	in clos ure	ex am ine
in her it	a pos tle	a base ment	dis cred it
des pot ic	con sist ent	a bate ment	re sult ant
be wil der	im pos tor	com pla cent	mag net ic
bap tis mal	la con ic	de po nent	ma jes tic

2	3	4	5	6	1	2	3	4	5	1	2	3	1
not	nor	move	done	wolf–	tube	tub	fur	full	rude–	type	hymn	myrrh–	new

LESSON 55.

Words of two syllables, accented on the first.

2	1	3	2
En′try	col′ter	bor′der	pip′pin
en ter	fo cus	cor ner	pig gin
er ror	glo ry	hor net	brig and
an vil	lo cust	mor tal	tin sel
ax is	mo ment	mor tar	tip pet
ed dy	po tent	mor bid	ed it
lat ter	sto ic	or chard	clos et
tat ter	sto len	hor ror	blot ter
pat ter	mo pish	ar mor	spot ted
tes ter	do tard	car go	vic ar
wit ty	do tage	tar dy	vom it
wit ness	du ring	par don	tan sy

LESSON 56.

Words of two syllables, accented on the first.

2	2	3	4
Ar′ro*w*	spar′ro*w*	bor′ro*w*	al′so
har ro*w*	el bo*w*	mor ro*w*	al der
mar ro*w*	bel lo*w*	sor ro*w*	al ter
nar ro*w*	fel lo*w*	bur ro*w*	wal nut
yar ro*w*	mel lo*w*	fur ro*w*	wal rus
hal lo*w*	yel lo*w*	bar ley	wal ter
sal lo*w*	bil lo*w*	par ley	fal ter
tal lo*w*	pil lo*w*	gar ment	pal try
shal lo*w*	wil lo*w*	tur key	bal sam
shad o*w*	win do*w*	fur nish	wa ter
cal lo*w*	win no*w*	or der	there fore
fal lo*w*	wid o*w*	or bit	where fore

LESSON 57.

Words of two syllables, accented on the second.

1	1	4	4
Con voke'	ac cuse'	bal loon'	car toon'
dis close	ad duce	bab oon	pol troon
dis pose	im pure	lam poon	sa loon
ver bose	re vive	bas soon	co coon
sup port	re vise	dra goon	shal loon
pro voke	com pile	pla toon	a loof
sup pose	im port	rac coon	be hoof
par take	af ford	har poon	be hoove
ar cade	re pose	fes toon	bam boo
cas cade	en force	mon soon	hal loo
cru sade	im pose	pon toon	re proof
in case	ex plore	buf foon	re prove

LESSON 58.

Words in which *gh*, *l*, *k*, and *w* are silent.

1	1	2	2	2
Ni*gh*	*w*hole	*k*nack	*w*rack	ba*l*m
hi*gh*	*w*rote	*k*nab	*w*rap	ca*l*m
si*gh*	*w*rite	*k*nag	*w*reck	pa*l*m
thi*gh*	*w*reak	*k*nap	*w*ren	*p*sa*l*m
fi*gh*t	*w*ray	*k*nell	*w*rench	a*l*ms
li*gh*t	*w*rithe	*k*nelt	*w*rest	ca*l*f
mi*gh*t	*w*reath	*k*nit	*w*retch	ha*l*f
ni*gh*t	*w*ry	*k*nob	*w*rig	4
ri*gh*t	*k*no*w*	*k*nock	*w*ring	ta*l*k
si*gh*t	*k*noll	*k*not	*w*rist	cha*l*k
hi*gh*t	*k*nee	*k*neck	*w*rit	wa*l*k
ti*gh*t	*k*nead	*k*nop	*w*rong	sta*l*k

LESSON 59.

WHAT I HATE TO SEE.

I hate to see an idle dunce,
  Who don't get up till eight,
Come slowly moping into school,
  A half an hour too late.

I hate to see his shabby dress;
  His buttons off his clothes;
With blacking on his hands and face,
  Instead of on his shoes.

I hate to see a scholar gape,
  And yawn upon his seat:
Or lay his head upon his desk,
  As if almost asleep.

I hate to see a boy so rude,
  That one might think him raised,
In some wild region of the woods,
  And but half civilized.

I hate to see a scholar's desk
  With toys and playthings full.
As if to play with rattle-traps.
  Were all he did at school.

I hate to see a shabby book,
  With half the leaves torn out,
And used as if its owner thought
  'Twas made to toss about.

1	2	3	4	5	1	2	3	4	1	2	3	4	1
fate	fat	far	fall	care—	mete	met	her	there—	pine	pin	sir	machine—	no

LESSON 60.

Words in which some of the letters are silent.

1	2	4	3	4
Beard	lamb	dawn	earth	shoe
crease	limb	fawn	earl	tomb
heave	crumb	lawn	earn	tour
greave	dumb	pawn	learn	soup
leave	numb	brawn	yearn	group
eaves	plumb	drawn	dearth	who
sheaf	thumb	bawl	heard	whom
shear	jamb	brawl	hearse	whose
folks	debt	drawl	pearl	whoop
comb	kemb	sprawl	search	balk
source	tempt	shawl	heart	calk
slow	kiln	hawk	guard	caul

LESSON 61.

Words of two syllables, accented on the first.

1	1	2	2
Bea′con	height′en	glad′den	christ′en
bea ver	light en	beck on	glist en
dea con	sweet en	heav en	list en
drear y	treat y	length en	fast en
ea ger	bra zen	reck on	drunk en
ea gle	maid en	crim son	kitch en
grea sy	shak en	pris on	chick en
mea gre	strait en	quick en	thick en
seam stress	tak en	smit ten	bit ten
mea sles	wak en	stif fen	driv en
squeam ish	weak en	swiv el	kit ten
year ling	ra ven	writ ten	silk en

LESSON 62.

Words of two syllables, accented on the first.

1	1	1	1
Dai′ly	bea′dle	tro′phy	free′man
dai sy	pea cock	oak um	keep sake
dain ty	rea son	yeo man	twee zers
cai tiff	sea son	shoul der	meet ing
tai lor	east ward	poul try	pee vish
prai rie	trea tise	poul tice	nee dle
fail ure	clear ance	isl and	lime kiln
ca lyx	treat ment	twi light	re gion
cha os	peo ple	vice roy	le gion
cho rus	pre cept	ci pher	stee ple
fra cas	cre dence	vi tals	flee cy
game ster	gree dy	ty phus	se rous

LESSON 63.

Words of one syllable.

1	1	1	ou	2
Beeves	sheep	plague	ounce	aunt
bleed	sleep	vague	flounce	daunt
breeze	sleeve	league	pounce	gaunt
cheer	sneer	rogue	gouge	haunt
cheese	sneeze	vogue	lounge	jaunt
creep	speech	brogue	ground	taunt
creek	spleen	fugue	plough	vaunt
fleece	squeeze	gourd	bough	flaunt
screech	wheeze	course	slough	launch
screen	steep	fourth	drought	staunch
seethe	freeze	mould	slouch	craunch
sheen	grease	moult	pouch	haunch

1 2 3 4 5 1 2 3 4 1 2 3 4 1
fate fat far fall care—mete met her there—pine pin sir machine—no

LESSON 64.

Words in which *th* has the soft or flat sound.

2	1	2	2
This	thy	baths	lath'er
that	tho*ugh*	laths	teth er
than	tithe	paths	we*a*th er
their	blithe	3	le*a*th er
them	lithe	fath'er	neth er
thus	*w*rithe	far thing	wheth er
thence	s*c*ythe	far ther	hith er
1	bathe	far thest	thith er
thine	lathe	bur then	prith ee
thee	soothe	5	whith er
these	smoothe	moth'er	both er
those	bre*a*the	broth er	fe*a*th er

LESSON 65.

Words of three syllables accented on the second.

2	2	2
A mend'ment	dis tem'per	Sep tem'ber
an gel ic	con tent ment	No vem ber
ap pen dix	pre sent ment	De cem ber
as sem bly	pu tres cent	re sent ment
at tend ant	in trep id	a bun dant
ath let ic	re fresh ment	a sun der
re plen ish	em bel lish	en cum ber
de mer it	em bez zle	ef ful gent
de pend ent	en gen der	re ful gent
di lem ma	en ven om	com pul sive
re mem ber	pre vent ive	tri um phant
re luc tant	qui es cent	re dun dant

2	3	4	5	6	1	2	3	4	5	1	2	3	1
not	nor	move	done	wolf–	tube	tub	fur	full	rude–	type	hymn	myrrh–	new

LESSON 66.

Words of three syllables, accented on the second.

1	1	1
Dic ta′tor	sub scrib′er	con fes′sor
tes ta′tor	de cri al	ag gres sor
cre a tor	un e qual	suc ces sor
bra va do	co e qual	trans fig ure
lum ba go	qui e tus	pre fig ure
vi ra go	il le gal	dis fig ure
far ra go	bi tu men	com mix ture
hi a tus	a cu men	con tin ue
in ci sor	le gu men	for bid ding
en vi ron	tri bu nal	con jec ture
pro vi so	pa go da	de ben ture
de ci pher	spec ta tor	in den ture

LESSON 67.

Words of three syllables, accented on the second.

2	2	2
Con tex′ture	ac com′plish	com mit′tee
en rap ture	ad mon ish	con sid er
un er ring	har mon ic	in trin sic
a quat ic	im pos ture	con tin gent
as sas sin	al lot ment	be nig nant
e las tic	nar cot ic	ac quit al
fan tas tic	car bon ic	de liv er
sar cas tic	ma son ic	di min ish
fa nat ic	a bol ish	dis trib ute
dra mat ic	em bod y	in sip id
de fal cate	pa cif ic	e nig ma
em phat ic	pro hib it	im bit ter

1 2 3 4 5 1 2 3 4 1 2 3 4 1
fate fat far fall care—mete met her there—pine pin sir machine—no

LESSON 68.

Words of three syllables accented on the third.

1	1	2
Ap per tain′	de com pose′	com pre hend′
as cer tain	re com pose	rep re hend
en ter tain	in ter pose	rec om mend
su per vene	pre dis pose	rep re sent
in ter vene	im po lite	rec ol lect
im por tune	re u nite	in ter cept
op por tune	dis u nite	in ter sect
in se cure	re in state	in ter mit
in ter fere	dis re pute	dis af fect
pre ma ture	in ter leave	in di rect
im ma ture	in ter weave	coun ter act
ad ver tise	mis be have	in ter dict

LESSON 69.

Words of three syllables accented on the third.

1	1	2
Su per scribe′	mis de mean′	ap pre hend
su per vise	un fore seen	cir cum vent
sub di vide	re ap pear	un der sell
co in cide	o ver reach	dis con tent
o ver drive	un de ceive	con de scend
un der mine	per se vere	in cor rect
cav al cade	in ter cede	con tra dict
can non ade	dis ap pear	in dis tinct
lem on ade	o ver leap	un der stand
ser e nade	o ver sleep	o ver hang
prom e nade	in tro duce	o ver match
bar ri cade	am a teur	vi o lin

2 3 4 5 6 1 2 3 4 5 1 2 3 1
not nor move done wolf—tube tub fur full rude—type hymn myrrh—new

LESSON 70.

Words of three syllables, accented on the first.

2	2	1
Ag′gran dize	bev′er age	fla′gran cy
as pi rate	im mi grate	va can cy
can di date	cal a bash	fra gran cy
con ju gate	par a dise	like li hood
ex ca vate	lex i con	mi cro scope
nav i gate	tem po ral	li bra ry
ven e rate	liv e ry	pli a ble
al i quot	bal us trade	di a lect
an ti pode	cher u bim	vi o lent
med ic al	dem o crat	vi o late
ep i gram	cap ri corn	ra di ate
ep i thet	daf fo dil	pri va cy

LESSON 71.

Words of three syllables, accented on the first.

2	3	2
Par′a phrase	per′ma nent	af′fluent
par a graph	ger mi nate	an ces tor
par al lax	ter mi nate	bal us ter
par al lel	ur gen cy	bar ris ter
mack er el	ser vi tude	car ri on
flat u lent	ver ti go	can is ter
sac ri lege	per fi dy	lav en der
den i zen	per ju ry	ac tu al
ep i cure	nurs e ry	ad ju tant
ep i sode	cor mo rant	al co ran
el e phant	cor por al	al ge bra
el e gant	cor pu lent	al ti tude

LESSON 72.

Words of three syllables, accented on the first.

2	2	2
Mag′ni tude	cin′na mon	mon′u ment
am pli tude	in stru ment	con fi dent
ag o nize	in tel lect	con ti nent
ap pe tite	in ter est	pop u lar
lat i tude	cit i zen	grad u ate
las si tude	min er al	fas ci nate
ac cu rate	min is ter	grav i tate
ac tu ate	sir i us	lac er ate
ag gra vate	stim u lus	pal li ate
ap pro bate	vin e gar	ab di cate
par o dy	bod i ly	ab ro gate
ar ro gate	com e dy	ad e quate

LESSON 73.

Words of three syllables accented on the first.

2	2	2
Pil′grim age	sen′ti ment	cel′e brate
stim u late	tes ta ment	pen e trate
dis si pate	ded i cate	em i grate
dis lo cate	des per ate	ex tri cate
lin e age	es ti mate	ex pi ate
big a my	des ti tute	reg u late
dil u ent	hab i tude	ren o vate
it er ate	el o quent	spec u late
im pe tus	ex cel lent	veg e tate
mil li ner	pes ti lent	con se crate
pol i ty	dec o rate	con vo cate
prob i ty	el e vate	ob du rate

2 3 4 5 6 1 2 3 4 5 1 2 3 1
not nor move done wolf-tube tub fur full rude-type hymn myrrh-new

LESSON 74.

Words of two syllables, accented on the first.

2	2	2	3
Latch'et	sol'em*n*	san'guin*e*	hard'ware
jack et	col um*n*	land scape	hard ship
fresh et	vol ume	spend thrift	tar nish
wick et	an s*w*er	brim stone	pars nip
crick et	con quer	trib une	star light
pock et	grand *eu*r	non su*i*t	cor sair
mus ket	mid ni*gh*t	mus lin	for feit
trip let	up ri*gh*t	wel kin	corse let
skil let	quag mire	pass age	horn pipe
off set	wind pipe	gab bl*e*	sur feit
trum pet	um pire	cac kl*e*	fur tive
doub let	vin*e* yard	tac kle	sar casm

LESSON 75.

Words of two syllables, in which *ph* has the sound of *f* and *ch* the sound of *k*.

2	1	2	2
Phil'ter	pha'lanx	cam'phor	chem'ist
phys ic	pha sis	pam phlet	chron ic
phan tom	phœ nix	dip*h* throng	chol ic
phon ic	si phon	trip*h* throng	schol ar
phos phate	hy phen	zeph yr	sched ule
phren sy	tri umph	sap phic	an arch
phan tasm	ca liph	sap phire	an chor
phe*a*s ant	pi broch	ser aph	ep och
soph ist	su mach	neph ew	ech o
spher ic	te trach	sul phur	pas chal
sul phate	cho ral	graph ic	strych nine

LESSON 76.

Words of two syllables, accented on the second.

1	2	2	1
Pro rogue′	har angue′	bur lesque′	a chieve′
pro vost	re lapse	gro tesque	ag grieve
re course	re venge	con demn	be lieve
re source	ag gress	be twixt	be siege
ap proach	con dense	be witch	re lieve
a dieu	de fence	e clipse	re prieve
ac crue	pre tence	in fringe	con ceive
im bue	im mense	in debt	de ceive
im pugn	be friend	a bridge	con ceit
be stow	bi sect	im pinge	per ceive
re new	sus pense	re scind	re ceipt
re view	sup press	re strict	re ceive

LESSON 77.

Words of two syllables, accented on the second.

1	1	1	1
An neal′	dis ease′	be seech′	in deed′
ap pear	dis please	be tween	pro ceed
ap pease	en dear	can teen	re deem
be neath	im peach	ca reer	set tee
be queath	mal treat	com peer	suc ceed
be speak	mis lead	dis creet	tu reen
be reave	de feat	es teem	un seen
bo h a	en treat	ex ceed	bre vier
con ceal	re lease	fore see	cash ier
con geal	re peal	fu see	fron tier
de feat	re treat	gen teel	re trieve
de cease	re veal	gran dee	de ceit

LESSON 78.

Words of two syllables, accented on the second.

4	4	2	1
Ap plaud'	ap pall'	be guile	es quire'
ap plause	be fall	be lie	sur mise
be cause	in stall	be nign	de prive
as sault	re call	de sign	de scribe
de fault	in thrall	as sign	de spise
ex haust	with al	de light	con dign
de fraud	ba salt	af fright	con sign
de bauch	ex alt	dis guise	ma lign
ba shaw	a thwart	chas tise	re sign
with draw	a ward	com prise	sub scribe
pa sha	re ward	in quire	es chew
pa paw	ma raud	sur prise	as tute

LESSON 79.

Words of two syllables, accented on the first.

1	1	2	1
Gait'er	like'wise	flex'ile	chief'tain
trait or	trea cle	plan tain	griev ance
way ward	neu tral	das tard	griev ous
pa geant	faith ful	trans cript	thiev ish
dia mond	youth ful	shep herd	ceil ing
light ning	hail stone	wres tle	eith er
por trait	righ ful	coup let	neith er
pro logue	states man	coup le	seiz ure
so journ	brain pan	trou ble	leis ure
nui sance	sea man	sal ver	crea ture
rhu barb	stew ard	mas tiff	fea ture
truth ful	vis count	jaun dice	weak ness

1 2 3 4 5 1 2 3 4 1 2 3 4 1
fate fat far fall care—mete met her there—pine pin sir machine—no

LESSON 80.

Words of three syllables, accented on the first.

2	2	2
Ban′ish ment	con′ti nent	Sat′ur day
rav ish ment	teg u ment	pol i cy
pun ish ment	char i ot	in fan cy
ped i ment	pol y glot	con stan cy
sed i ment	an te past	clem en cy
com pli ment	in ter est	sum ma ry
lin i ment	pen te cost	land la dy
mer ri ment	par a dox	mel o dy
det ri ment	hol i day	pros o dy
sen ti ment	car a way	mon o dy
doc u ment	leg a cy	bat ter y
mon u ment	fal la cy	flat u lence

LESSON 81.

Words of three syllables, accented on the second.

1	2	2
De port′ment	at tach′ment	mo nas′tic
ex po nent	a ban don	or gan ic
e lope ment	ap par el	pe dan tic
op po nent	at lan tic	ro man tic
pro mo tive	bo tan ic	ty ran nic
pro po sal	dog mat ic	com pen sate
a bu sive	ec stat ic	con tem plate
ac cu sant	es tab lish	in tes tate
a muse ment	pris mat ic	ap pen dant
cher u bic	gi gan tic	nar cis sus
in duce ment	in hab it	re pub lic
re fu sal	me tal ic	ex cul pate

2	3	4	5	6	1	2	3	4	5	1	2	3	1
not	nor	move	done	wolf	tube	tub	fur	full	rude	type	hymn	myrrh	new

LESSON 82.

Words of three syllables, accented on the first.

2	2	2
Ev'i dent	prac'ti cal	can'ni bal
eb o ny	gran a ry	am nes ty
ef fi gy	gal le ry	cal um ny
em bas sy	cas si mere	ar ro gant
em i nent	an ec dote	fac to ry
em e rald	sen ti nel	par a sol
ex o dus	ref lu ent	tab u lar
fel o ny	res i dent	slip per y
gen e sis	rev er ent	sym pa thy
lep ro sy	rev er end	typ i cal
men di cant	ad mi ral	vir u lent
pen i tent	al co hol	but ter y

LESSON 83.

Words of three syllables, accented on the first.

2	2	2
Pan'to mime	cam'o mile	sanc'ti fy
car a van	pal pi tate	sas sa fras
ad a mant	tran quil ize	sat ir ize
as ter isk	sub se quent	par a site
clar i fy	can o py	scar i fy
cran ber ry	cat a ract	sat el lite
cav al ry	cat a pult	chas ti ty
mar i gold	pat ron ize	cal cu late
tam a rind	tes ti fy	ul cer ate
vag a bond	sub stan tive	cul ti vate
mar i time	mul ti tude	mus cu lar
am ber gris	sub sti tute	pub li can

1 2 3 4 5 1 2 3 4 1 2 3 4 1
fate fat far fall care—mete met her there—pine pin sir machine—no

LESSON 84.

BATTLE OF FORT MOULTRIE.

Among the earliest battles during the contest with England for American Independence, was the gallant defence of Fort Moultrie.

This fort was on an island, at the mouth of Charleston harbor, in South Caralina. It was a rough fort, built of palmetto logs. But though the fort was rough, it had some brave men within it. And bravely did they defend it, against a whole fleet of the enemy's ships. So well did they return the fire, that the enemy was glad to escape, with the loss of many men and much damage to their ships.

Twelve of the brave men in the fort were killed, and a much larger number were wounded by the balls fired from the ships. The flag under which they fought was the flag of South Carolina,—a blue flag, with a crescent, or half moon, in white.

This was but one of the many battles which were fought, and these brave men were but a small part of the many thousands who gave their lives, that our country might be free and happy; and that we might be at liberty to make our own laws. And now when you think of breaking any of the laws of your country, stop and think what it cost to make them.

2 3 4 5 6 1 2 3 4 5 1 2 3 1
not nor move done wolf—tube tub fur full rude—type hymn myrrh—new

LESSON 85.

Words of three syllables, accented on the second.

3	4	ou
A part'ment	de fault'er	a bound'ing
ca thar tic	hy draul ic	ac count ant
to ma to	ma raud er	an nounce ment
de ter mine	tar paul'ing	as tound ing
pre fer ment	ex haust er	de nounce ment
in ter pret	de bauch ment	es pou sal
fra ter nal	ap plaud ing	en coun ter
dis burse ment	as sault ing	ren counter
a bor tive	ex alt ing	pro nounc ing
dis or der	with draw al	sur round ing
im mor tal	ap prov al	pro found ly
re cord er	re mov al	dis mount ed

LESSON 86.

Words of three syllables, accented on the second.

1	1	1
Ac quaint'ance	as sign'ment	re fine'ment
ap prais er	a sy lum	re quire ment
as sail ant	ac quire ment	com pi ler
at tain der	en light en	re li ance
com plain ant	en liv en	sa li va
re main der	ex cite ment	com pli ance
cour a geous	in dict ment	con ni vance
out ra geous	in cite ment	af fi ance
con ceal ment	de fi ance	un fad ing
de mean or	dis ci ple	vice ge rent
e gre gious	ob tru sive	a mu sing
in vei gle	il lu sive	dif fu sive

LESSON 87.

Words of three syllables, accented on the third.

1	4	1
Brig a dier′	trans ma rine′	moun tain eer′
cav a lier	sub ma rine	pri va teer
chev a lier	bom ba zine	mu ti neer
fi nan cier	mag a zine	o ver seer
gren a dier	man da rine	en gin eer
cap a pie	quar an tine	vol un teer
chan de lier	tam bou rine	buc ca neer
can on ier	pal an quin	pi o neer
car bin ier	cap u chin	auc tion eer
cor de lier	mis im prove	gaz et teer
gon do lier	re in stall	mu le teer
bom bar dier	o ver awe	ruf u gee

LESSON 88.

Words of four syllables, accented on the first.

1	2	2
Lu′mi na ry	del′i ca cy	cus′tom a ry
cu li na ry	con tu ma cy	hon or a ry
mo nien ta ry	ac cu ra cy	mil li ner y
nu ga to ry	com pe ten cy	sem i na ry
nu me ra ry	im po ten cy	pul mo na ry
bre vi a ry	nec es sa ry	lit er a ry
a mi a ble	ig no min y	ad ver sa ry
fa vor a ble	cer e mo ny	cem e ter y
va ri a ble	mat ri mo ny	sol i ta ry
nu mer a ble	pat ri mo ny	vol un ta ry
su per a ble	tes ti mo ny	trib u ta ry
du bi ta ble	an ti qua ry	sump tu a ry

LESSON 89.

Words of four syllables, accented on the first.

2	2	2
Com'mis sa ry	dif'fi cul ty	sal'a man der
mon as ter y	ex i gen cy	cap il la ry
ob du ra cy	pres by ter y	max il la ry
ob sti na cy	pun ish a ble	jan i za ry
oc cu pan cy	vul ner a ble	stat u a ry
cor ol la ry	ut ter a ble	ap o plex y
con tro ver sy	suf fer a ble	ter ri to ry
an ti mo ny	in ven to ry	ex cre to ry
al a bas ter	pur ga to ry	prom is so ry
cat ter pil lar	man da to ry	in ti ma cy
mag is tra cy	al le go ry	im i ta tive
spec u la tor	or a to ry	im i ta ble

LESSON 90.

Words of four syllables, accented on the second.

2	2	2
Ac com'mo date	pro cras'ti nate	re trib'u tive
a mal ga mate	con grat u late	con ser va tive
com men su rate	e jac u late	de fin i tive
a dul ter ate	e man ci pate	con sec u tive
e lab o rate	e rad i cate	ex ec u tive
cor rob o rate	e vap o rate	de mon stra tive
di lap i date	tri en ni al	de riv a tive
de bil i tate	mil len ni al	in fin i tive
in tox i cate	per en ni al	di min u tive
fa cil i tate	sep ten ni al	ter res tri al
in fat u ate	sex ten ni al	col lat ter al
in val i date	bi en ni al	con di tion al

LESSON 91.

ANALYSIS.

Where is the accent in *Commissary?* It is on the first syllable.

What is the sound of the vowel in the accented syllable? It is the short sound, marked by the figure 2.

How is the long sound of a vowel marked?—By the figure 1. What are the vowel sounds denoted by 3, 4, 5, and 6?

How many sounds has the consonant *c*? It has two, the hard like *k*, and the soft like *s*.

Which sound has it in *Commissary?* The hard.

Before what letters is it always hard? Before *a*, *o*, *u*, *l*, *r*, and *t*.

Before what letters is it always soft? Before *e*, *i*, and *y*.

How many sounds has *s*? Two, the sharp as in *hiss*, and the flat, as in *his*.

Which has it here? The sharp.

What sound has *a* in the third syllable? The long sound.

Are words ever accented on more than one syllable? Yes, they sometimes have what is called a secondary accent.

Where is the secondary accent in *Commissary?* On the third syllable.

2 3 4 5 6 1 2 3 4 5 1 2 2 1
not nor move done wolf-tube tub fur full rude-type hymn myrrh new

LESSON 92.

Words of four syllables, accented on the second.

1	2	2
O be'di ent	ex trav'a gant	an tag'o nist
ma te ri al	in sen si ble	a nat o mist
un eas i ness	in tem per ate	au dac i ty
con ve ni ent	ex pen sive ly	bar bar i ty
anx i e ty	in con stan cy	ca lam i ty
a dor a ble	im pas sa ble	a nal o gy
un u su al	be at i tude	a nat o my
in ju ri ous	ca tas tro phe	a nal y sis
im me di ate	es tab lish ment	ca lam i tous
ex ceed ing ly	a ban don ment	mi rac u lous
va ri e ty	a cad e my	cer ti fi cate
o be di ence	a lac ri ty	e quiv o cate

LESSGN 93.

Words of four syllables, accented on the third

1	2	1
Cir cum ja'cent	ad o les'cent	pre en gage'ment
re in force ment	al pha bet ic	en ter tain ment
af fi da vit	ar gu ment al	in de ci sive
an te ce dent	com pli ment al	mis de mean or
mus co va do	con ti nent al	ap pa ra tus
bas ti na do	mon u ment al	per se ver ance
in co he rent	sac ra ment al	su per vi sor
des per a do	sen ti ment al	en gin eer ing
me di a tor	ep i lep tic	dis a gree ment
mau so le um	ef fer ves cent	un der ta ker
in ter fer ence	ep i dem ic	vir tu o so
ju ris pru dence	ap o plec tic	pan a ce a

LESSON 94.

Words of four syllables, accented on the third.

2	2	2
Dem o crat'ic	con va les'cent	com pre hen'sive
mem o ran dum	in de pend ent	fun da ment al
ad a man tine	cor res pond ent	in u en do
ar ma dil lo	ap os tol ic	man i fes to
ben e fac tor	sys tem at ic	o ver shad *ow*
mal e fac tor	hor i zon tal	in ter mit tent
math e mat ics	in stru ment al	be a tif ic
ac a dem ic	or na ment al	pan e gyr ic
dis en cum ber	dis a vow al	met a phys ic
pred e ces sor	o ri ent al	dis con tent ment
in ter ces sor	par e gor ic	par a lyt ic
ev a nes cent	phil o soph ic	sci en tif ic

LESSON 95.

Words of three syllables, accented on the first.

2	2	1
Hom'i cide	scan'dal ize	di'a gram
par i cide	sol em nize	di o cese
sac ri fice	stig ma tize	vi a duct
al ka li	sym bol ize	si ne cure
er u dite	syl lo gize	du te *ous*
gal van ize	sub si dize	a que *ous*
gor man dize	tan ta lize	du bi *ous*
mag net ize	tem po rize	te di *ous*
mor al ize	can on ize	o di *ous*
or gan ize	civ il ize	*eu* pho ny
pul ver ize	col o nize	ne o phite
rec og nize	crys tal ize	pha e ton

2 3 4 5 6 1 2 3 4 5 1 2 3 4
not nor move done wolf-tube tub fur full rude-type hymn myrrh-new

LESSON 96.

Words of three syllables, accented on the first.

1	2	2
Stu′di *ous*	hid′e *ous*	haz′ard *ous*
co pi *ous*	in fa m*o*us	vil l*ai*n *ous*
se ri *ous*	em u l*o*us	mem bran *ous*
glo ri *ous*	gen er *ous*	ran cor *ous*
cu ri *ous*	pros per *ous*	sul phur *ous*
fu ri *ous*	rig or *ous*	ven tur *ous*
spu ri *ous*	slan der *ous*	rap tur *ous*
glu ti n*o*us	clam or *ous*	mis ch*i*ev *ous*
lu mi n*o*us	rav en *ous*	stren u *ous*
lu di cr*o*us	pon der *ous*	sin u *ous*
dan ger *ous*	mur der *ous*	tyr an n*o*us
mu ti n*o*us	vig or *ous*	ul cer *ous*

LESSON 97.

Words of three syllables, accented on the first.

1	2	2
Fu′mi gate	cat′e chise	crim′i nal
pu tre fy	mach in ate	dis so nant
for ger y	sac cha rine	id i om
gro cer y	at mos phere	cim e ter
o di um	ab la tive	in ter val
o pi um	af fa bl*e*	min is try
fo li age	im ple ment	chem i cal
fo li o	beg gar y	el o quence
mu ti late	ex ple tive	her i tage
nu mer al	plen ti ful	ver i ly
pu ri tan	skel e ton	tel e scope
de cen cy	ven i son	neg a tive

1 2 3 4 5 1 2 3 4 1 2 3 4 1
fate fat far fall care—mete met her there—pine pin sir machine—no

LESSON 98.

Words of three syllables, accented on the first.

2	2	3
Blas'phe my	bac'cha nal	phar'ma cy
aph o rism	bron chi al	harp si chord
em pha sis	an arch y	ar chi trave
ep i taph	an chor age	ar che type
hem i sphere	al che my	ar chi tect
lith o graph	lach ry mal	car pen ter
met a phor	in cho ate	mar ma lade
phos pho rus	mech an ism	part ner ship
proph e cy	mich ael mas	mar gin al
soph is try	pen ta teuch	har mo nize
soph o more	sep ul chre	har di hood
spher i cal	syn chro nism	mar ket house

LESSON 99.

Words of four syllables, accented on the second.

1	1	2
Col le'gi ate	pos te'ri or	ca pac'i ty
a e ri al	spon ta ne ous	com par a tive
an nu i ty	lux u ri ous	con cav i ty
me mo ri al	col lu so ry	di ag o nal
e lu ci date	tra ge di an	fa tal i ty
ex co ri ate	tor tu i tous	fru gal i ty
in fu ri ate	pro pri e tor	hu man i ty
ac cu mu late	com e di an	in hab it ant
mer cu ri al	ad ju di cate	di am e ter
en co mi um	ag glu ti nate	hi lar i ty
bar ba ri an	en thu si ast	lo cal i ty
gram ma ri an	re du pli cate	lo quac i ty

2	3	4	5	6	1	2	3	4	5	1	2	3	1
not	nor	move	done	wolf–tube	tub	fur,	full	rude–type	hymn	myrrh	–new		

LESSON 100.

Words of four syllables, accented on the second.

2	2	1
Fan tas′ti cal	fa nat′i cism	re mu′ner ate
for mal i ty	a nath e ma	ef flu vi um
le gal i ty	i tal i cize	vi tu per ate
e van gel ize	chi mer i cal	sa lu bri ty
e van gel ist	com plex i ty	par tu ri ent
men dac i ty	com mis ser ate	ab ste mi *ous*
mis an thro py	ne ces si tate	lu gu bri *ous*
ol fac to ry	as sev er ate	le gu mi nous
o rac u lar	ex tem po re	me lo di *ous*
pre par a tive	vo rac i ty	cen so ri *ous*
ras cal i ty	ex as per ate	com mu ni ty
dis par age ment	ex hil er ate	im pu ni ty

LESSON 101.

Words of four syllables, accented on the second.

2	2	2
Bel lig′er ent	re cip′ro cate	hy poth′e nuse
con sis ten cy	ob liq ui ty	e mol u ment
con tin gen cy	po lyg a my	or thog ra phy
a ris to crat	re frig er ate	pre dom i nate
cen trif u gal	re lin quish ment	ther mom e ter
con viv i al	so phis ti cal	bi og ra pher
de lin quen cy	ven tril o quism	his tor i cal
e pit o me	ven tril o quist	par tic i pate
dis crim i nate	e con o mize	pub lic i ty
ha bit u ate	ge ol o gist	fe roc i ty
in fin i ty	phi lol o gy	du plic i ty
in sin u ate	phi los o phy	mu nic i pal

LESSON 102.

Words of four syllables, accented on the first.

2	2	3
Prof′it a ble	val′u a ble	spec′u la tive
tol er a ble	hon or a ble	ex pli ca tive
ad mi ra ble	hos pi ta ble	cop u la tive
an swer a ble	hab i ta ble	fig u ra tive
char i ta ble	cred i ta ble	nom i na tive
fash ion a ble	des pi ca ble	op per a tive
lem en ta ble	en vi a ble	sep a ra tive
mar riage a ble	es ti ma ble	im i ta tive
nav i ga ble	eq ui ta ble	fed er a tive
prac ti ca ble	per ish a ble	pal li a tive
van quish a ble	ex e cra ble	med i ca tive
con quer a ble	pon der a ble	med i ta tive

LESSON 103.

Words of four syllables, accented on the first.

2	2	2
Spir′it u al	tem′per a ture	jes′u it ism
lin e a ment	car i ca ture	ep i cu rism
tem per a ment	lit er a ture	min er al ist
nec ro man cy	ag ri cul ture	pros e lyt ism
des ul to ry	hor ti cul ture	vol a til ize
vis ion a ble	cal cu la tor	pit i a ble
mis sion a ry	com men ta tor	prom on to ry
dic tion a ry	mod er a tor	cas u ist ry
sta tion a ry	nav i ga tor	es tu a ry
men di can cy	ven ti la tor	am a to ry
pres i den cy	reg u la tor	al i mo ny
flat u len cy	in sti ga tor	in ven to ry

2 3 4 5 6 1 2 3 4 5 1 2 3 1
not nor move done wolf—tube tub fur full rude—type hymn myrrh—new

LESSON 104.

Words of three syllables accented on the first.

2	2	1
Mem'o ry	dem'a gogue	di'a logue
mes sen ger	ped a gogue	eu cha rist
mas to don	dec a logue	aid de camp
man u mit	cat a logue	bay o net
flat u lence	ap o logue	suit a ble
ec sta cy	am e thyst	cham ber lain
her e tic	hyp o crite	pleu ri sy
quer u lous	syc a more	main te nance
mez zo tint	sym me try	pa geant ry
ret ro gade	syn o nym	trai tor ous
priv i lege	sym pho ny	a pri cot
vir u lent	syl la bub	ru di ment

LESSON 105.

Words of three syllables, accented on the second.

1	2	3
En slave'ment	en camp'ment	ad journ'ment
a maze ment	scho las tic	ob serv ant
un eas y	con cen tric	sub ver sive
ar rear age	me theg lin	in cur sive
en treat y	por ten tous	in dorse ment
be reave ment	hys ter ic	pre serv er
be he moth	en fran chise	re vers al
pro ceed ings	con tin gence	ex tir pate
co he sive	clan des tine	un bur den
ad he sive	in stinct ive	u surp er
in tru sive	en chant ment	trans verse ly
col lu sive	dis as trous	in per fect

LESSON 106.

Words of three syllables, in which *ti* has the sound of *sh*.

2	1	1
Ab duc'tion	for ma'tion	vi bra'tion
ab strac tion	gra da tion	va ca tion
a dop tion	lo ca tion	do na tion
af flic tion	mi gra tion	dic ta tion
as sump tion	mu ta tion	ces sa tion
at ten tion	trans la tion	cre a tion
col lec tion	nar ra tion	col la tion
con cep tion	plan ta tion	ab lu tion
con sump tion	pri va tion	di lu tion
con ven tion	pro ba tion	pol lu tion
con vic tion	vo ca tion	so lu tion
cor rup tion	e qua tion	de vo tion

LESSON 107.

Words of three syllables, in which *ti* has the sound of *sh*.

2	1	2
De trac'tion	foun da'tion	at ten'tion
dis trac tion	frus tra tion	pro trac tion
de cep tion	ne ga tion	per cep tion
de duc tion	pul sa tion	ob jec tion
de jec tion	re la tion	pro duc tion
de fec tion	sal va tion	con ten tion
in struc tion	e mo tion	cor rec tion
pre sump tion	se cre tion	de ten tion
re duc tion	ap por tion	e lec tion
am bi tion	com mo tion	di rec tion
con tri tion	de ple tion	per fec tion
fru i tion	pro por tion	in flec tion

LESSON 108.

Words of three syllables, in which *si* has the sound of *sh*.

Ac ces'sion	di gres'sion	sup pres'sion
ad mis sion	dis cus sion	trans gres sion
ag gres sion	ex pan sion	per cus sion
as cen sion	ex pul sion	re pul sion
com mis sion	ex ten sion	sub mis sion
com pres sion	ex pres sion	con cus sion
com pul sion	pos ses sion	o mis sion
con fes sion	di men sion	per mis sion
con ces sion	pre ten sion	im pres sion
con vul sion	pro gres sion	pro fes sion
de clen sion	re mis sion	trans mis sion
de pres sion	se ces sion	dis mis sion

LESSON 109.

Words in which *ci* and *ti* have the sound of *sh*.

De fi'cient	op ti'cian	ex pa'ti ate
ef fi cient	pa tri cian	in sa ti ate
pro fi cient	phy si cian	in gra ti ate
suf fi cient	ma gi cian	ne go ti ate
om ni scient	po ten tial	as so ciate
ju di cial	pru den tial	de pre ci ate
of fi cial	sub stan tial	dis so ci ate
pro vin cial	in i tial	e ma ci ate
fi nan cial	sol sti tial	ex cru ci ate
es pe cial	es sen tial	ap pre ci ate
lo gi cian		
mu si cian	com mer cial	sub stan ti ate

2 3 4 5 1 2 3 4 1 2 3 4 1
ate fat far fall care—mete met her there—pine pin sir machine—no

LESSON 110.

Words in which *ce*, *ci* and *ti* have the sound of *sh*.

1	2	1
'a pa'cious	au spi'cious	lo qua'cious
u da cious	ca pri cious	men da cious
al la cious	ju di cious	te na cious
e ro cious	ma li cious	pre co cious
er ba ceous	de li cious	sa ga cious
rus ta ceous	per ni cious	fa ce tious
es ta ceous	sus pi cious	vex a tious
i tro cious	of fi cious	2
o ra cious	nu tri tious	con ten tious
vi va cious	am bi tious	sen ten tious
e ra cious	fic ti tious	in fec tious
a pa cious	fac ti tious	li cen tious

LESSON 111.

Words in which *ti*, *si* and *ci* have the sound of *sh*.

3	2	1
As ser'tion	mu ni'tion	a ca'cia
de ser tion	vo li tion	ro ta tion
in ser tion	tra di tion	tax a tion
dis tor tion	re stric tion	re ple tion
ab sorp tion	pre dic tion	pro ca cious
a ver sion	mi li tia	se qua cious
con ver sion	si fi cious	in fla tion
dis per sion	com pas sion	stag na tion
im mer sion	sus pen sion	quo ta tion
in ver sion	suc ces sion	pro mo tion
co er cion	op pres sion	temp ta tion
im par tial	im pul sion	car na tion

2 3 4 5 6 1 2 3 4 5 1 2 3
not nor move done wolf–tube tub fur full rude–type hymn myrrh–new

LESSON 112.

Words of four syllables, accented on the second.

2	2	
A pol′o gy	ad min′is ter	de pop′u late
bi og ra phy	ar til le ry	a pol o gize
chro nol o gy	sim plic i ty	cos mop o lite
ge og ra phy	sub lim i ty	the od o lite
ma hog a ny	scur ril i ty	in oc u late
lith og ra phy	de liv er ance	de rog a tive
meth od i cal	con glom er ate	de moc ra cy
me trop o lis	con sol i date	dox ol o gy
the ol o gy	pre pon der ate	con cat e nate
the oc ra cy	ex post u late	com pet i tor
to pog ra phy	prog nos ti cate	con trib u tor
zo ol o gy	ap prox i mate	ex pos i tor

LESSON 113.

Words of four syllables, accented on the second.

2	2	1
Ad ven′tu rous	tem pest′u *ous*	bi tu′mi nous
a non y mous	in gen u *ous*	gra tu i tous
mag nan i mous	con tin u *ous*	pe nu ri *ous*
as par a gus	pro mis cu *ous*	sa lu bri ous
in vid i *ous*	mel lif lu *ous*	sul phu re *ous*
as sid u *ous*	con spic u *ous*	er ro ne *ous*
con tig u *ous*	am phib i *ous*	com mo di *ous*
tu mul tu *ous*	car niv o rous	fe lo ni *ous*
vo lup tu *ous*	ge lat i nous	op pro bri *ous*
ca lum ni *ous*	pre pos ter *ous*	pre ca ri *ous*
su per flu *ous*	il lus tri *ous*	gre ga ri *ous*
in dus tri *ous*	in dec o rus	ne fa ri *ous*

1 2 3 4 5 1 2 3 4 1 2 3 4 1
fate fat far fall care—mete met her there—pine pin sir machine—no

LESSON 114.

Words of four syllables, accented on the second.

2	1	3
Com pul'so ry	an nu'i tant	ex ter'mi nate
in cum ben cy	com mu ni cant	e mer gen cy
re dun dan cy	im mu ni ty	pre serv a tive
re luc tant ly	in fu ri ate	pro ver bi al
re ful gen cy	com mu ni cate	su per flu *o*us
pe nult i mate	mer cu ri al	ab surd i ty
tri um vi rate	pro tu ber ance	re turn a ble
com bus ti ble	con cu pis cence	su per la tive
cor rupt i ble	fa tu i ty	fra ter ni ty
in flam ma ble	gra tu i ty	di ver si fy
im pres si ble	im pu ri ty	sub ser vi ent
de mon stra ble	dis qui et ude	in cor po rate

LESSON 115.

Words of three syllables, accented on the first.

2	2	2
Ser'a phim	christ'en dom	mag'net ism
prej u dice	hin der ance	lex i con
cham pi on	lic o rice	vig il ance
im pu dence	pen i tence	chan cel lor
pref er ence	spec ta cle	dul ci mer
met a phor	tre*a*ch er *o*us	suf fo cate
con quer or	tre*a*ch er y	sub ter fuge
bach e lor	rev er ence	sup pu rate
in ter course	in di gence	ful mi nate
priv i lege	in so lence	in ter stice
r*h*et o ric	prim i tive	in sti tute
hec a tom*b*	sim ple ton	con se quence

2 3 4 5 6 1 2 3 4 5 1 2 3 1
not nor move done wolf—tube tub fur full rude—type hymn myrrh—new

LESSON 116.

Words of three syllables, accented on the first.

1	2	3
Cham'ber lain	cog'ni zance	jour'nal ist
di a phragm	con gru ence	cour te sy
re qui em	chron i cle	tur bu lence
me te or	hon es ty	per vi ous
u ni corn	scrof u lous	per ti nence
truth ful ly	ab sti nence	ar mis tice
hi e rarch	log a rithm	charge a ble
hy dro gen	mon arch y	mar vel ous
night in gale	ob se quies	myr mi don
tith a ble	ox y gen	por phy ry
me di um	peas ant ry	por cu pine
ni tro gen	jeal ous y	por rin ger

LESSON 117.

Words of three syllables, accented on the first.

4	ou	2
Laud'a ble	coun'ter pose	quack'er y
laud a num	coun ter march	rhap so dy
au di ence	coun ter sign	par a mour
au thor ize	coun ter feit	af flu ence
plau si ble	coun te nance	an arch y
au di tor	boun ti ful	aph o rism
talk a tive	boun te ous	aq ue duct
wa ter fall	boun da ry	den tis try
wa ter man	doubt ful ly	neg li gence
al ma nac	foun der y	fem i nine
mov a ble	moun tain ous	her o ine
fool er y	moun te bank	jeop ard y

LESSON 118.

Words of four syllables, in which *ti* has the sound of *sh*.

1	1	1
Ab di ca'tion	cal cu la'tion	ed u ca'tion
ac cla ma tion	ar bi tra tion	ex cla ma tion
ac cu sa tion	cel e bra tion	en er va tion
af fir ma tion	com bi na tion	ex pec ta tion
ag gra va tion	com mu ta tion	fas ci na tion
ded i ca tion	com pen sa tion	hab i ta tion
de fal ca tion	con fla gra tion	hes i ta tion
del e ga tion	con se cra tion	an nex a tion
dep u ta tion	cul ti va tion	cir cu la tion
des o la tion	dis pu ta tion	con fis ca tion
au pu ta tion	dev as ta tion	con fu ta tion
ab so lu tion	dis ser ta tion	con ju ga tion

LESSON 119.

Words of four syllables, in which *ti* has the sound of *sh*.

1	2	1
Dem on stra'tion	ab o li'tion	con tri bu'tion
dec la ma tion	ac qui si tion	con sti tu tion
em i gra tion	am mu ni tion	des ti tu tion
ex ca va tion	com pe ti tion	dim i nu tion
gen e ra tion	com po si tion	dis so lu tion
grav i ta tion	def i ni tion	dis tri bu tion
il lus tra tion	dis po si tion	el o cu tion
im pli ca tion	ben e dic tion	in sti tu tion
in for ma tion	con tra dic tion	per se cu tion
lim i ta tion	rec og ni tion	res o lu tion
lit i ga tion	op po si tion	res ti tu tion
mod u la tion	pro hi bi tion	rev o lu tion

2 3 4 5 6 1 2 3 4 5 1 2 3 1
not nor move done wolf–tube tub fur full rude–type hymn myrrh–new

LESSON 120.

Words of four syllables, in which *ci* **and** *ti* **have the sound of** *sh.*

2	2	1
Ar ti fi′cial	rev er en′tial	con tu ma′cious
ben e fi cial	un sub stan tial	ef fi ca′cious
su per fi cial	pes ti len tial	per ti na cious
prej u di cial	un es sen tial	per spi ca cious
un of fi cial	pres i den tial	per pe tra tion
pol i ti cian	in flu en tial	pres en ta tion
*rh*et o ri cian	av a ri cious	pub li ca tion
con se quen tial	in ju di cious	mas ti ca tion
con fi den tial	in au spi cious	nav i ga tion
pen i ten tial	in ef fi cient	sal u ta tion
prov i den tial	in suf fi cient	rec re a tion

LESSON 121.

Words of four syllables, accented on the second.

1	2	2
Ap proach′a ble	as tron′o my	im pov′er ish
ap pro pri ate	in dem ni ty	phe nom e non
col lo qui al	com mod i ty	ab dom i nal
har mo ni ous	con com i tant	sym bol i cal
con trol la ble	the at ri cal	pre rog a tive
re stor a tive	dis syl la ble	re spon si ble
de plor a ble	pre cip i tous	*rh*i noc e ros
no to ri ous	em pyr e al	sy non y mous
di plo ma cy	pre cip i tance	i dol a trous
pro pri e ty	as ton ish ment	me trop o lis
as sign a ble	*ch*ro nom e ter	an gel i cal
so bri e ty	hy poth e sis	mo not o nous

1 2 3 4 5 1 2 3 4 1 2 3 4 1
fate fat far fall care—mete met her there—pine pin sir machine—no

LESSON 122.

WHO IS MY NEIGHBOR? LUKE X. 29—36.

But he, willing to justify himself, said unto Jesus, And who is my neighbor?

And Jesus, answering, said, A certain man went down from Jerusalem to Jericho, and fell among thieves, which stripped him of his raiment, and wounded him, and departed, leaving him half dead.

And, by chance, there came down a certain priest that way; and when he saw him, he passed by on the other side.

And likewise a Levite, when he was at the place, came and looked on him, and passed by on the other side.

But a certain Samaritan, as he journeyed, came where he was; and when he saw him he had compassion on him,

And went to him, and bound up his wounds, pouring in oil and wine, and set him on his own beast, and brought him to an inn, and took care of him.

And on the morrow, when he departed, he took out two pence, and gave them to the host, and said unto him, Take care of him; and whatsoever thou spendeth more, when I come again I will repay thee.

Which, now, of these three, thinkest thou, was neighbor unto him that fell among the thieves?

And he said, He that shewed mercy on him.

2 3 4 5 6 1 2 3 4 5 1 2 3 1
not nor move done wolf—tube tub fur full rude—type hymn myrrh new

LESSON 123.

Words of four syllables, accented on the second.

1	2	2
Al le′gi ance	in her′i tance	in tan′gi ble
*ch*a me le on	e ques tri an	su prem a cy
in gre di ent	de pen den cy	as cen den cy
si de re al	nu mer i cal	im preg na ble
im pe ri al	mo nas ti cism	pa ren the sis
op pro bri um	me rid i an	de gen e rate
in e bri ate	pe des tri an	in vig o rate
an ni hi late	ex trav a gance	le git i mate
e the re al	phi lan thro py	in vin ci ble
chi ca ne ry	ver nac u lar	o rig i nate
in clin a ble	som nam bu list	pro pin qui ty
ad vi so ry	*ch*a lyb e ate	so phis ti cate

LESSON 124.

Words of four syllables, accented on the second.

3	3	4
Im per′ti nent	im mor′tal ize	im prov′a ble
con vert i ble	con form a ble	im mov a ble
im per vi *ou*s	de form i ty	ap prov ing ly
ad ver bi al	im por tu nate	buf foon e ry
de ter mi nate	con form i ty	co coon e ry
e ter ni ty	ac cord ing ly	ac *cou* tre ment
im per fect ly	e nor mi ty	ap pall ing ly
pa ter ni ty	co part ner ship	ex h*au*st i ble
ad ver si ty	im par tial ly	de b*au*ch e ry
al ter na tive	im firm i ty	in *au* gu rate
di ver si ty	af firm a tive	in *au* di ble
con ser va tive	re turn a ble	ma chin er y

1 2 3 4 5 1 2 3 4 1 2 3 4 1
ate fat far fall care—mete met her there—pine pin sir machine—no

LESSON 125.

Words of four syllables, accented on the third.

2	2	2
As tro nom′ic	the o crat′ic	ap pre hen′sive
cal vin is tic	con va les cence	per ad ven ture
cat e gor ic	co a les cence	man u fac ture
ac qui es cence	om ni pres ence	su per struc ture
phi lan throp ic	ef flo res cence	ju ris dic tion
cir cum spec tion	at mos pher ic	di a lec tic
hem i spher ic	pred e ces sor	ty po graph ic
hy po thet ic	reg i ment al	bi o graph ic
dip lo mat ic	rep re hen sive	em blem at ic
ac ci dent al	ret ro spec tive	syc o phan tic
det ri ment al	sym pa thet ic	ef fer ves cence
met a phor ic	an a lyt ic	rem i nis cence

LESSON 126.

Words of four syllables, accented on the third.

2	2	2
Ap pre hen′sion	prep o si′tion	pu ri tan′ic
com pre hen sion	ex hi bi tion	e nig mat ic
con de scen sion	prop o si tion	ar o mat ic
in ter ces sion	sup po si tion	un ex pect ed
in ter mis sion	su per sti tion	un con nect ed
man u mis sion	rep e ti tion	mu ri at ic
rep re hen sion	hyp o crit ic	sup ple ment al
in ter ven tion	syl lo gis tic	or na ment al
su per vi sion	cal o rif ic	the o ret ic
ap pa ra tion	id i ot ic	par en thet ic
ap po si tion	pe ri od ic	in ci dent al
pre mo ni tion	e co nom ic	the o log ic

2 3 4 5 6 1 2 3 4 5 1 ~2 3
not nor move done wolf tube tub fur full rude–type hymn myrrh–ne

LESSON 127.

Words of four syllables, accented on the first.

2	2	2
Prot′est ant ism	min′er al ize	trans′i to ry
prop a gand ism	prod i gal ize	ac ri mo ny
ped a gog ism	sec u lar ize	im i ta tor
par a sit ism	sen su al ize	el i gi ble
pol y the ism	al co hol ize	spir it u *ou*-
par al lel ism	an i mal ize	3
phar i see ism	al le go rize	par′don a b
gen er al ize	char ac ter ize	par si mo n
lib er al ize	cul ti va tor	ar bi tra ry
nat u ral ize	dil a to ry	mer ce na r
ox y gen ize	mon i to ry	dor mi to r
pop u lar ize	pred a to ry	or di na ry

LESSON 128.

Words of five syllables, accented on the second.

2	2	1
Ap pel′la to ry	vo lup′tu a ry	in du′bi ta ble
con sol a to ry	re pos i to ry	gra tu i t*ou*s l
de fam a to ry	de clar a to ry	ma te ri al ize
pre par a to ry	ex plan a to ry	in va ri a ble
de rog a to ry	pro hib it o ry	pe cu ni a ry
sub sid i a ry	con fed er a cy	in nu mer a bl
e pis to la ry	in del i ca cy	o be di ent ly
vo cab u la ry	he red i ta ry	pe nu ri *ou*s ly
in vol un ta ry	de gen er a cy	no to ri *ou*s ly
re sid u a ry	in vet e ra cy	me lo di *ou*s ly
tu mult u a ry	le git i ma cy	la bo ri *ou*s ly
im ag in a ry	e pis co pa cy	me mo ri al ist

1 2 3 4 5 1 2 3 4 1 2 3 4 1
fate fat far fall care—mete met her there—pine pin sir machine—no

LESSON 129.

Words of five syllables, accented on the third.

1	2	2
Am bi gu'i ty	prod i gal'i ty	flex i bil'i ty
im por tu ni ty	pop u lar i ty	in sip id i ty
su per flu i ty	per son al'i ty	sen si bil i ty
in cre du li ty	joc u lar i ty	an i mos i ty
in se cu ri ty	lib er al i ty	me di oc ri ty
op por tu ni ty	sin gu lar i ty	sec u lar i ty
in ge nu i ty	im mo ral i ty	du ra bil i ty
im ma tu ri ty	sen su al i ty	mu ta bil i ty
con ti nu i ty	sol u bil i ty	val e dic to ry
per spi cu i ty	tan gi bil i ty	u na mim i ty
as si du i ty	vis i bil i ty	vol a til i ty
con tra ri e ty	im be cil i ty	rec i proc i ty

LESSON 130.

Words of four syllables, accented on the second.

2	2	2
Ma lev'o lent	co in'ci dent	ob lit'e rate
im prov i dent	mu nif i cent	hy poc ri sy
in dif fer ent	an tith e sis	de spond en cy
om nip o tent	a rith me tic	mo nop o ly
ste ril i ty	ac cliv i ty	ba rom e ter
ma lig ni ty	ac tiv i ty	ver bos i ty
so lil o quy	af fin i ty	ty pog ra phy
re cip i ent	an tiq ui ty	ste nog ra phy
e pis co pal	a gil i ty	phle bot o my
e quiv a lent	pon tif i cate	a poc ry phal
pre dom i nant	si mil i tude	e piph a ny
om nip o tence	vi cis si tude	e phem e ral

2	3	4	5	6	1	2	3	4	5	1	2	3	1
not	nor	move	done	wolf–	tube	tub	fur	full	rude–	type	hymn	myrrh–	new

LESSON 131.

Words of four syllables, accented on the second.

1	2	2
A gra′ri an	de gen′e rate	ef fem′i nate
pal la di um	do mes ti cate	pro pen si ty
cu ta ne *ous*	ex pec to rate	com pres si ble
ter res que *ous*	in ter ro gate	con vex i ty
as sa*i*l a ble	in ves ti gate	de test a ble
ob ta*i*n a ble	in vet er ate	ac cept a ble
sec ta ri an	vul gar i ty	ap pel la tive
re stra*i*n a ble	ty ran ni cal	in tel li gent
mys te ri *ous*	ex ten u ate	po et i cal
ob se qui *ous*	aus ter i ty	pro gen i tor
col le gi an	de crep i tude	pe des tri an
a gree a ble	re spec tive ly	im men si ty

LESSON 132.

Words of four syllables, accented on the second.

2	2
Dis fran′chise ment	En fran′chise men t
com mend a ble	pro phet ic al
ac com plish ment	in quis i tive
re cep ta cle	as ton ish ment
em bel lish ment	a*c* *k*no*w*l edge ment
per plex i ty	sar coph a gus
ag gran dise ment	phy lac ter y
em bar rass ment	ha bil i ment
ap pren tice ship	som nam bu lism
em bez zle ment	im pris on ment
con tem pla tive	an tag o nism
sym met ri cal	in teg u ment

1 2 3 4 5 1 2 3 4 1 2 3 4 1
fate fat far fall care—mete met her there—pine pin sir machine—no

LESSON 133.

Words of five syllables, accented on the second.

2	2
Com mem'o ra ble	con fec'tion a ry
a bom i na ble	dis pen sa to ry
in ev i ta ble	ex clam a to ry
in sep a ra ble	ex tem po ra ry
in ex o ra ble	in cen di a ry
in ex pli ca ble	sti pen di a ry
in im i ta ble	pre lim i na ry
con sid er a ble	ef fem i na cy
in hab it a ble	in flam ma to ry
in vul ner a ble	un nec es sa ry
co tem po ra ry	pre mon i to ry
de clam a to ry	in hab i tan cy

LESSON 134.

Words of five syllables, accented on the second.

3	2
Im per'me a ble	com mem'o ra tive
in ter mi na ble	a poth e ca ry
im per ti nent ly	o bit u a ry
im per vi a ble	dis crim i na tive
un ser vice a ble	de lib er a tive
un mer chant a ble	pre cip i tan cy
ob ser va to ry	in ex tri ca ble
con serv a to ry	ir rep a ra ble
sub ser vi en cy	ac com pa ni ment
un for tu nate ly	in quis i tive ly
ex or bi tant ly	im per a tive ly
im por tu nate ly	com par a tive ly

LESSON 135.

Words of five syllables, accented on the third.

2	1
Con san guin'i ty	in ter me'di ate
per pen dic u lar	mag is te ri al
in di vid u al	dis o be di ent
in ar ti cu late	in ex pe di ent
il le git i mate	mat ri mo ni al
con tra dic to ry	tes ti mo ni al
er y sip e las	im me mo ri al
in tel lec tu al	pat ri mo ni al
in ef fect u al	dis pro por tion ate
in sig nif i cant	in con sol a ble
phil o soph i cal	in sup port a ble
phil o log i cal	e qua to ri al

LESSON 136.

Words of five syllables, accented on the third.

1	2
Im ma te'ri al	cir cum am'bi ent
an ti mo ni al	e qui pon der ate
cer e mo ni al	im mor tal i ty
ter ri to ri al	phys i ol o gy
par si mo ni ous	trig o nom e try
or a to ri o	in tro duc to ry
im pro pri e ty	cor di al i ty
rec on cil a ble	dem o crat i cal
no to ri e ty	hos pi tal i ty
con ti gu i ty	prin ci pal i ty
ex com mu ni cate	en er get i cal
per pe tu i ty	rep re sen ta tive

LESSON 137.

Words of five syllables, accented on the fourth.

1	2
Ad min is tra′tor	ex per i men′tal
dis ad van ta *geo*us	a pol o get ic
per e gri na tion	a man u en sis
glo ri fi ca tion	su per in tend ent
in ter po la tion	mis ap pre hen sion
sanc ti fi ca tion	ar is to crat ic
ab bre vi a tion	en thu si as tic
ad ju di ca tion	ec cle si as tic
ad min is tra tion	hi e ro glyph ic
al lit er a tion	sar sa pa ril la
a mal ga ma tion	math e ma ti cian
e lec tion eer ing	mis un der stand ing

LESSON 138.

Words of five syllables, accented on the fourth.

1	1
Am pli fi ca′tion	mul ti pli ca′tion
ap pro pri a tion	or gan i za tion
as sas si na tion	pro cras ti na tion
as sim i la tion	pro nun ci a tion
clas si fi ca tion	ram i fi ca tion
col o ni za tion	cor rob o ra tion
com mis er a tion	e quiv o ca tion
con fed er a tion	per am bu la tion
in car cer a tion	qual i fi ca tion
in oc u la tion	ex ten u a tion
in ter ro ga tion	sol em ni za tion
cir cum lo cu tion	trans fig u ra tion

2 3 4 5 6 1 2 3 4 5 1 2 3 1
not nor move done wolf-tube tub fur full rude-type hymn myrrh-new

LESSON 139.

Words of five syllables, accented on the third.

Bi o graph'i cal (2)	pu sil lan'i mous (2)
cos mo graph i cal	car a van sa ry
ge o graph i cal	sym pa thet i cal
math e mat i cal	e qui lat e ral
to po graph i cal	su per an u ate
ac a dem i cal	em blem at i cal
ty po graph i cal	par al lel o gram
al pha bet i cal	min er al o gy
ar gu ment a tive	gen e al o gy
cat e chet i cal	sat is fac to ry
e van gel i cal	sim i lar i ty
ge o met ri cal	crim i nal i ty

LESSON 140.

Words of five syllables, accented on the third.

Met a phor'i cal (3)	man u fac'to ry (2)
met a mor pho sis	reg u lar i ty
non con form i ty	gen e ral i ty
u ni form i ty	di a met ri cal
in de ter mi nate	el e ment a ry
con tro vert i ble	ap os tol i cal
an ni ver sa ry	phra se ol o gy
u ni ver sal ist	mag na nim i ty
un re ver si ble	sup ple ment a ry
u ni ver si ty	an a tom i cal
tac i tur ni ty	an i mos i ty
al le gor i cal	ar is toc ra cy

1 2 3 4 5 1 2 3 4 1 2 3 4 1
fate fat far fall care—mete met her there—pine pin sir machine—no

LESSON 141.

Words of five syllables, accented on the third.

2	2
Deu ter on'o my	met a phys'i cal
e co nom i cal	af fa bil i ty
et y mol o gy	rec ti lin e al
in ter rog a tive	prob a bil i ty
gen er os i ty	o dor if er ous
lex i cog ra pher	pos si bil i ty
as tro nom i cal	mul ti plic i ty
par a dox i cal	in tre pid i ty
pe ri od i cal	fal li bil i ty
hyp o chon dri ac	e lec tric i ty
cu ri os i ty	ec cen tric i ty
e qui pon der ant	ca pa bil i ty

LESSON 142.

Words of five syllables, accented on the third.

1	2
Pres by te'ri an	meth od ist'i cal
min is te ri al	au then tic i ty
ep i cu re an	gram i niv o rous
in con gru i ty	ab o rig i nes
mul ti tu di *nous*	in di vid u al
del e te ri *ous*	car ti lag i *nous*
ho mo ge ne *ous*	mu ci lag i *nous*
lon gi tu di nal	ge o log i cal
cer e mo ni *ous*	zo o log i cal
in stan ta ne *ous*	at mos pher i cal
mis cel la ne *ous*	hem i spher i cal
si mul ta ne *ous*	ar chi pel a go

LESSON 143.

Words of five syllables, accented on the fourth.

1	2
Rep re sen ta′tion	char ac ter is′tic
sig ni fi ca tion	en to mo log ic
e man ci pa tion	ep i gram mat ic
e vap o ra tion	gen e a log ic
ges tic u la tion	lex i co graph ic
re ver ber a tion	mon o syl lab ic
ver si fi ca tion	or ni tho log ic
re cip ro ca tion	os te o log ic
in ter pre ta tion	phys i o log ic
ex am i na tion	ich thy o log ic
or gan i za tion	per i pa tet ic
ad min is tra tion	su per in ten dence

LESSON 144.

Words of six syllables accented on the fourth.

1	2
Ad min is tra′tor ship	ac çount a″bil′i ty
pre des ti na ri an	ap pli ca bil i ty
sex a ge na ri an	com pat i bil i ty
dis ci pli na ri an	com pres si bil i ty
par a pher na li a	di vis i bil i ty
ex tem po ra ne *ous*	el i gi bil i ty
het e ro ge ne *ous*	con viv i al i ty
en cy clo pæ di a	in stru men tal i ty
gu ber na to ri al	ma te ri al i ty
me di a to ri al	mu nic i pal i ty
in quis i to ri al	u ni ver sal i ty
an te di lu vi an	il lib er al i ty

LESSON 145.

Words of six syllables, accented on the fourth.

Ar is to cratʹi cal
con ge ni al i ty
en thu si as ti cal
in hos pi tal i ty
spir it u al i ty
pen e tra bil i ty
im prob a bil i ty
im pla ca bil i ty
mal le a bil i ty
gen e ral is si mo
me te or ol o gy
gen e a log i cal

in flam ma bilʹi ty
in ca pa bil i ty
im mu ta bil i ty
il leg i bil i ty
re fran gi bil i ty
in fal li bil i ty
in sen si bil i ty
im pos si bil i ty
de struc ti bil i ty
per cep ti bil i ty
de fen si bil i ty
com bus ti bil i ty

LESSON 146.

Words of six syllables, accented on the fourth.

Med i ter raʹne an
co tem po ra ne ous
dis ad van ta geous ly

in flex i bil i ty
re sist i bil i ty
in cred i bil i ty
re spect a bil i ty
re spon si bil i ty
dis sim i lar i ty
par tic u lar i ty
ir reg u lar i ty

ex per i mentʹal ly
trig o no met ri cal
et y mo log i cal
ec cle si as ti cal
prac ti ca bil i ty
im pet u os i ty
pro por tion al i ty
a pol o get i cal

in con tro vertʹi ble
in fe ri or i ty
su pe ri or i ty

2 3 4 5 6 1 2 3 4 5 1 2 3 1
not nor move done wolf-tube tub fur full rude-type hymn myrrh-new

LESSON 147.

Words of seven syllables, accented on the fifth.

Per pen dic u lar'i ty	in com pres si bil'i ty
im ma te ri al i ty	in de fen si bil i ty
in di vid u al i ty	in tel li gi bil i ty
in tel lec tu al i ty	in sur mount a bil i ty
in di vis i bil i ty	me te or o log i cal
in com pat i bil i ty	im prac ti ca bil i ty
in de struc ti bil i ty	im mal le a bil i ty
im per cep ti bil i ty	in va ri a bil i ty
ir re sist i bil i ty	in con ge ni al i ty
in com bus ti bil i ty	
im pen e tra bil i ty	val e tu di na'ri an
in el i gi bil i ty	an ti trin i ta ri an

LESSON 148.

Words to be divided into their proper syllables.

Bod'ily	drop'sical	ho'liness
bottomless	jocular	soberly
commoner	jollity	glorify
document	butterfly	notary
confident	cultivate	notional
continent	customer	various
impudent	publisher	violent
impotent	summary	funeral
indicate	ossify	fumigate
indigent	providence	finery
infamy	robbery	radius
insolent	sorrowful	duteous

LESSON 149.

Words to be divided into their proper syllables.

2	2	2
Nul'lify	mar'tyrdom	cin'namon
mulberry	barbarism	simpleton
multiply	particle	lavender
solvency	porcupine	scavenger
monitor	origin	ligament
politics	orrery	globular
senator	porphyry	management
idiom	vertigo	testament
minister	terminus	fellowship
bachelor	pervious	capsular
myrmidom	harbinger	prevalent
syllogism	arduous	provident

LESSON 150.

Words to be divided into their proper syllables.

2	2	1
Insin'uate	fig'urative	accum'ulate
illiterate	tributary	communicate
invidious	sedentary	intuitive
invincible	veritable	luxurious
contributor	statuary	unusual
consolidate	catepillar	obscurity
depopulate	acrimony	credulity
discordancy	dilatory	occasional
intolerance	emissary	proportional
emolument	critically	notorious
preponderate	inventory	indecency
inconstancy	radically	obedient

LESSON 151.

Words to be divided into their proper syllables.

1	2	2
Modula'tion	manufac'ture	antic'ipate
numeration	agriculture	duplicity
ordination	horticulture	audacity
propagation	superstructure	municipal
publication	atmospheric	publicity
transportation	diplomatic	atrocity
tribulation	theoretic	sagacity
suppuration	insufficient	velocity
undulation	opposition	solicitude
visitation	prohibition	participate
ventilation	repetition	solicitor
reservation	effervescent	medicinal

LESSON 152.

Words to be divided into their proper syllables and properly accented.

Epidemical	plausibility	countryman
testimonial	register	paragraph
perpetuity	compasses	daughter
effeminacy	vegetate	sprinkling
homogenial	chronometer	toothache
residuary	compassion	parchment
justifiable	tetrarch	unpopular
incendiary	persecute	contagious
longitudinal	excitement	outrageous
dictatorial	anarchy	distinguish
confederacy	camomile	enormity
pennyweight	handkerchief	obliquity

LESSON 153.

JUST WHAT HE WAS, WHEN A BOY.

A few evenings since, while slowly making my exit from a crowded lecture-room, where an appreciative audience had been listening with absorbed interest to the glowing pictures of India, presented by a popular and gifted lecturer, an earnest voice by my side exclaimed :

"Just what he was when he was a boy. I heard him offer his first praye in public, and I shall never forget my feelings. He was just as earnest then as now."

"But," said a lady in reply, "can you belive all he has said ?"

"Yes," was the instant reply. "That boy could never say what was not exactly true. I beleive him just as much as I believe the Bible."

I mused upon the words, "Just what he was when a boy." The same quick thoughts, glowing with poetic imagery—the same fervid eloquence seemed to lift the hearer to some lofty stand-point, whence the far-famed luxuriance of Eastern climes stretches out a sea of verdure before his admiring gaze, or amid this oriental grandeur of scenery sees the vast crowds held in thraldom of debasing errors, till his heart grows to stretch forth his hand to those perishing millions, and pluck them as "brands from the burning."

Oh, that these carelessly uttered words might

have fallen upon the heart of every boy in our land, making each realize that even now he is weaving the mantle of his future manhood, tracing his character in dim outline, to which future years shall only add the shading! How wise then, in youth, to follow noble ambitions, to do those things which are right!

LESSON 154.

Words of irregular pronunciation.

Written.	*Pronounced.*	*Written.*	*Pronounced.*
Beau	bo	a ny	en'ny
beaux	bōze	bu ry	ber ry
says	sex	bu sy	biz zy
been	bin	bu reau	bu ro
choir	quire	Eng lish	ing lish
corps	core	flam beau	flam bo
once	wuns	col o nel	kur nel
ewe	yu	ew er	yu er
cough	kauf	haut boy	ho boy
draught	draft	de pot	de po
hough	hok	bis cuit	bis kit
laugh	laf	a gain	a gen'
lieu	lu	dis cern	diz zern
rough	ruf	e nough	e nuf
dough	do	rou deau	rou do
phlegm	flem	bat eau	bat o
bough	bou	vig nette	vin yet
slough	slou	ca tarrh	ca tar
slough	sluf	ca noe	ca noo

1 2 3 4 5 1 2 3 4 1 2 3 4 1
fate fat far fall care—mete met her there—pine pin sir machine—no

LESSON 155.

Words of irregular pronunciation.

Written.	*Pronounced.*	*Written.*	*Pronounced.*
Tough	tuf	quad drille	ca dril′
trough	trof	ga zette	ga zet
done	dun	bru nette	bru net
schism	sizm	hic cough	hik′up
pique	peek	iron	i urn
masque	mask	bu si ness	biz nes
does	duz		
caulk	kawk	lieu ten ant	lu ten′ant

LESSON 156.

Words in which *ei* has the sound of *a* long, and *aught* and *ought* have the sound of *awt*.

Frei*gh*t	dei*g*n	caught	ought
ei*gh*t	fei*g*n	faught	bought
slei*gh*	seine	naught	fought
wei*gh*	nei*gh*h	taught	thought
wei*gh*t	feint	haught	brought
rei*g*n	in vei*gh*	naught′y	*w*rought
skein	nei*gh*′bor	haught y	sought
rein	hein ous	daugh ter	naught

LESSON 157.

DERIVATIVE WORDS.

A Derivative is a word that is formed from some other word, by adding one or more syllables to it. Thus, from the word love, we have *lover*, *loved*, *loving*, *lovely*, *unloved*, *unlovely*.

The part thus added to the end of a word is called an *affix*.

2	3	4	5	6	1	2	3	4	5	1	2	3	1
not	nor	move	done	wolf-	tube	tub	fur	full	rude-	type	hymn	myrrh-	new

When placed at the beginning of a word it is called a *prefix.*

The principal of these affixes and prefixes with their definitions are given in the following tables:

TABLE OF AFFIXES.

ER—*the person who*,—as, *baker*, the person who bakes.
OR—*the person who*,—as, *inventor*, the person who invents.
ED—*did*,—as, *desired*, did desire.
ING—*continuing to*,—as, *running*, continuing to run.
FUL—*full of*,—as, *careful*, full of care
LY—*in a manner*,—as, *faithfully*, in a faithful manner.
LESS—*without*,—as, *faultless*, without fault.
ABLE—*that may be*,—as, *valuable*, that may be valuable.
IBLE—*that may be*,—as, *corruptible*, that may be corrupted.
NESS,—*state or quality*,—as, *neatness*, the state of being neat.
ISH—*somewhat*,—as, *blackish*, somewhat black.

LESSON 158.

TABLE OF PREFIXES.

UN—*not*,—as, *unlearned*, not learned.
IN—*not*,—as *indecent*, not necent.
DIS—*not to, not*,—as, *displease*, not to please.
DE—*from*,—as, *detract*, to take from.
DE—*down*,—as, *depress*, to press down.
EX—*out*,—as, *expell*, to drive out.
CON—*together*,—as, *contract* to draw together.
RE—*repetition*,—as, *reprint*, to print again.
MIS—*wrong*,—as, *miscount*, to count wrong.
UP—*upward*,—as, *upheave*, to heave upward.
OUT—*beyond*,—as, *outlive*, to live beyond.

COUNTER—*against*,—as, *counteract*, to act against.
SEMI—*half*—as, *semitone*, half a tone.
SUPER—*above*,—as, *supernatural*, above natural.
INTER—*among*,—as, *intermix*, to mix among.
PER—*through*, as, *pervade*, to go through.
POST—*after*,—as, *postscript*, written after.
PRE—*before*,—as, *prejudge*, to judge before.
PRO—*forth*,—as, *produce*, to bring forth.
FORE—*before*,—as, *foretell*, to tell before.

LESSON 159.

THE PLURAL OF NOUNS.

Among the simplest class of affixes are those which form the plural of nouns.

Rules for forming the plural.

1. The plural of most nouns is formed by adding *s* to the singular; as, boy, boys.
2. When *s* added to a word would be hard to pronounce *es* is added; as, lash, lashes; fox, foxes.
3. To render the union of sound easier, *f* and *fe* are changed into *ves*; as, wife, wives.
4. A few nouns form their plurals by changing the vowel: as, man, men.
5. *Y*, with a consonant before it, is changed into *ies*; as, fly, flies. Ox adds *en*; ox, oxen.

EXAMPLES OF PLURAL DERIVATIVES.

Sing.	*Plu.*	*Sing.*	*Plu.*	*Sing.*	*Plu.*
2	2	1	1	1	1
Bag	bags	babe	babes	beef	beeves
lamp	lamps	cane	canes	sheaf	sheaves
clock	clocks	flame	flames	knife	knives
pond	ponds	scale	scales	wife	wives
duck	ducks	tray	trays	loaf	loaves

2 3 5 5 6 1 2 3 4 5 1 2 3 1
not nor move done wolf–tube tub tur full rude–type hymn myrrh–new

Sing.	*Plu.*	*Sing.*	*Plu.*	*Sing.*	*Plu.*
2	2	2	2	ou	2
Half	halves	bench	bench'es	mouse	mice
calf	calves	dish	dish es	1	2
1	1	tax	tax es	child	children
sky	skies	match	match es	2	2
fly	flies	1	1	man	men
la'dy	la'dies	breeze	breez'es	woman	women
po ny	po nies	cheese	chees es	ox	oxen
cry	cries	spice	spi ces		

LESSON 160.

RULES FOR THE FORMATION OF DERIVATIVES.

I. Words of one syllable, and words accented on the last syllable, when they end with a single consonant, preceded by a single vowel, double the final consonant before an additional syllable that begins with a vowel; as, rob, robber.

EXCEPTIONS. *X*, *z* and *k* are never doubled.

2. A final consonant, when it is not preceeded by a single vowel, or when the accent is not on the last syllable, remains single before an additional syllable; as, toil, toiling; visit, visiting.

3. Words ending with any double letter, preserve it double before any additional termination not beginning with the same letter; as, see, seeing; hill, hilly.

4. Words ending with any double letter, preserve it double in all words formed by means of prefixes; as, spell, misspell.

5. Primitive words ending in a silent *e*, omit *e* before an additional syllable beginning with a vowel: as, remove, removal; take, taking.

EXCEPTIONS. Words ending in *ce* or *ge* retain the *e*

1	2	3	4	5	1	2	3	4	1	2	3	4	1
fate	fat	far	fall	care—	mete	met	her	there—	pine	pin	sir	machine—	no

before *able* or *ous*; as, trace, traceable. The *e* is retained in verbs ending in *oe* and *ee*; as, shoe, shoeing; see, seei ng.

6. Primitive words ending in *e* silent, usually retain it before an additional syllable beginning with a consonant; as, pale, paleness.

EXCEPTIONS. Awful, argument, abridgmet, duly, truly, acknowledgment, judgment, wholly, &c.

7. Primitive words ending in *y*, preceded by a consonant, change the *y* into *i* before any termination but *e* or one commencing with *i*; as, pity, pitiless.

EXCEPTIONS. The *y* is retained before words derived from *dry* and *shy*; as, dryness, shyness.

8. Primitive words ending in *y*, preceded by a vowel, do not change the *y* into *i*; as, joy, joyful.

EXCEPTIONS. Daily, laid, paid, said, &c.

9. Compound words usually retain the spelling of the words that compose them; as, horse-man, shell-fish.

EXCEPTIONS. In permanent compounds, or in derivative words, of which they are not the *roots*, the words *full* and *all* drop one *l*; as, handful; in temporary compounds they retain both; as, all-wise. When used as a prefix *miss* drops one *s*.

N. B. There are other exceptions to some of these rules too numerous to be introduced into an elementary book on Orthography. It is therefore left to the teacher to point them out, or direct the pupil to such sources as will give him the desired information.

The rules given above are sufficient to enable the pupil to spell most of the derivative words in the language, when he has learned the orthography of the primitives from which they are derived.

2 3 4 5 6 1 2 3 4 5 1 2 3 1
not nor move done wolt-tube tub fur full rude-type hymn myrrh-new

LESSON 161.

EXAMPLES UNDER RULE 1.

2	2	2	2
Bid	bid′ding	hot	hot′ter
wed	wed ding	rag	rag ged
rub	rub bing	clan	clan nish
rob	rob bing	sin	sin ner
blot	blot ting	tin	tin ner
drop	drop ping	beg	beg gar
dip	dip p ng	rob	rob ber
dig	dig ging	fop	fop pish
plan	plan ning	hog	hog gish

EXAMPLES UNDER RULE 2.

1	1	2	2
Che*a*t	che*a*t′ing	vis′it	vis′it ing
ra*i*n	ra*i*n ing	cav il	cav il ing
he*a*r	he*a*r ing	ut ter	ut ter ing
te*a*ch	te*a*ch ing	ex pand′	ex pand ing
pre*a*ch	pre*a*ch ing	con sent	con sent ing
la′bor	la′bor ing	e vent	e vent ful
fla vor	fla vor ing	in vent	in vent ed
mo*u*ld er	mo*u*ld er ing	pre tend	pre tend er
fe ver	fe ver ish	ex pend	ex pend ing

EXAMPLES UNDER RULE 3.

1	1	1	1
See	see′ing	bliss	blis′ful
free	fre dom	stiff	stiff ly
flee	flee ing	skill	skill ful
tree	tree less	will	will ful
glee	glee ful	still	still ness
stroll	stroll er	spill	spill ing

LESSON 162.

EXAMPLES UNDER RULE 4.

4	4	2	2
Call	mis call'	add	su per add'
stall	fore stall	mass	a mass
fall	be fall	pass	re pass
thrall	in thrall	fill	re fill
2	2	sell	un der sell
spell	mis spell	stuff	re stuff
press	de press	miss	re miss
tell	fore tell	cross	re cross
swell	over swell	dress	un dress

EXAMPLES UNDER RULE 5.

1	1	1	1
Ride	rid'ing	a wake'	a wak'en
bride	bri dal	in flame	in flam ing
take	tak ing	pa rade	pa rad ing
make	mak ing	de fame	de fam er
name	nam ing	ex cuse	ex cus ing
cure	cu ra ble	a muse	a muse ment
blame	blam a ble	ex plode	ex plod ing
guide	guid ing	a buse	a bus ive
fame	fam ous	cor rode	cor ro ding

EXAMPLES UNDER RULE 6.

1	1	1	1
Pale	pale'ness	hope	hope'ful
tame	tame ness	game	game ster
blame	blame less	shame	shame ful
name	name less	waste	waste ful
taste	taste less	love	love ly
lame	lame ness	wake	wake ful

2 3 4 5 6 1 2 3 4 5 1 2 3 1
not nor move done wolf tube tub fur full rude type hymn myrrh new

LESSON 163.

EXAMPLES UNDER RULE 7.

2	2	1	1
Ver'y	ver'i ly	speed'y	speed'i ly
heav y	heav i ly	eas y	eas i ly
read y	read i ly	might y	might i ly
stead y	stead i ly	hast y	has ti ly
hap py	hap pi ness	la zy	la zi ness
an gry	an gri ly	ho ly	ho li ness
cost ly	cost li ness	wea ry	wea ri ness
god ly	god li ness	sha dy	sha di ness
ug ly	ug li ness	jui cy	jui ci ness

EXAMPLES UNDER RULE 8.

oy	oy	1	1
Boy	boy'hood	play	play'ful
coy	coy ness	gay	gay ly
joy	joy ful	gray	gray ness
toy	toy ish	clay	clay ey
cloy	cloy ish	bray	bray er

EXAMPLES UNDER RULE 9.

1	1	2
Hail'stone	boat'man	bed'room
safe guard	gold smith	break fast
whale bone	load stone	hedge hog
bee hive	oat meal	pen knife
keep sake	rope walk	hand work
knee pan	snow drop	land lord
bride groom	sports man	sand stone
fire wood	luke warm	black smith
light house	key stone	block head
lime kiln	free hold	milk maid

1 2 3 4 5 1 2 3 4 1 2 3 4 1
fate fat far fall care—mete met her there—pine pin sir machine—no

LESSON 164.

EXAMPLES UNDER RULE 9.

2	1	4
Spell'ing book	pa'per mill	school'mas ter
pep per mint	ta ble cloth	fool har dy
ev er green	tale bear er	wa ter fowl
gen tle man	din ing room	wa ter man
bed cham ber	no ble man	la*w* su*i*t
han*d* ker chi*e*f	ju ry man	ward robe
can dle stick	no bod y	war fare
cop y book	base vi ol	3
but ter nut		horse man
musk mel on	cler'gy man	con sta*l*k
hum ming bird	fur ther more	char co*a*l
but ter milk	jour ney man	harts horn

LESSON 165.

Words formed by adding the affixes, *er* and *or*.

1	2	1	2
Dre*a*m'er	bank'er	cre a'tor	of fend'er
le*a*d er	plant er	dic ta tor	tor ment or
pre*a*ch er	hunt er	nar ra tor	con duct or
spe*a*k er	giv er	trans la tor	ag gress or
te*a*ch er	liv er	re deem er	a veng er
wa*i*t er	smug gler	ad vi ser	3
ra*i*l er	b*u*ild er	re fin er	in dors'er
dri ver	act or	di vid er	re cord er
bo*a*st er	think er	sur vi vor	re form er
mo*u*rn er	lodg er	op po ser	de sert er
*w*ri ter	mock er	sup port er	dis turb er
ru ler	rock er	con sum er	u surp er

LESSON 166.

Words in which the *e* in *ed* is silent.

1	2	oi	1
Blazed	filled	broiled	be reaved'
drained	lived	coiled	be sieged
hailed	dodged	foiled	ac quired
lamed	lodged	oiled	ad mired
paved	solved	soiled	ad vised
raised	4	toiled	ar rived
saved	called	ow	bap tized
feared	galled	bowed	com bined
steered	hauled	crowned	de prived
crowed	mauled	drowned	a dored
flowed	warmed	frowned	a bused
showed	warned	plowed	ac cused
snowed	moved	1	a mused
tuned	proved	a vailed'	con fused
4	5	de famed	oy
begged	loved	ap peared	de coyed
wedged	shoved	be lieved	en joyed

In words like the following, *d* is sometimes pronounced as *t*.

1	2	1	2
Braced	flashed	a based'	at tacked'
faced	fixed	es caped	con fessed
graced	mixed	em braced	dis pensed
laced	boxed	im peached	op pressed
scraped	locked	in creased	con vinced
traced	passed	en ticed	dis missed
2	classed	en grossed	ou
cracked	3	en forced	de nounced
dashed	marked	in duced	pro nounced

1 2 3 4 5 1 2 3 4 1 2 3 4 1
fate fat far fall care—mete met her there—pine pin sir machine—no

LESSON 167.

Words formed by prefixing *de*, *dis* and *ex*.

1	3	1	2
De grade′	dis charge′	ex claim′	ex pect′
de fame	dis arm	ex ceed	ex empt
de cry	de form	ex clude	ex pel
dis please	de part	ex change	dis cred it
dis place	de bar	ex hale	dis mem ber
dis grace	2	ex hume	dis hon est
dis like	dis band	ex ude	dis man tle
dis own	dis trust	ex pire	dis pir it

Words formed by prefixing *in* and *un*. *In* often becomes *im*, *il*, or *ir*, for the sake of sound.

2	1	1
In ac′tive	im pa′tient	in vi′o late
un hap py	un aid ed	in ca pa ble
un thank ful	un a ble	in cu ra ble
in clem ent	un fad ing	un du ti ful
un friend ly	un fail ing	un u su al
un health y	un faith ful	ir ra′di ate
im mod est	il le gal	il lu mi nate
im mor′al	in de cent	2
im prop er	un e qual	in ad′e quate
in con stant	un mind′ful	in fal li ble
in sol vent	un ho ly	in trans i tive
un com mon	un so cial	un nat u ral
un god ly	un time ly	im pen i tent
ir rup tion	im pru dent	in cred i ble
il lic it	in hu man	in def i nite
il lus trate	un e ven	in del i cate
un trod den	un sta ble	ir res o lute

LESSON 168.

Words formed by prefixing *con*, *mis*, and *re*. *Con* is sometimes changed into *com* or *col*.

2	1	1	2
Con tract′	re claim′	mis be have′	re com mit′
con vert	re place	mis re late	re an nex
com press	re mind	mis be lieve	re in vest
col lect	com pose	mis ap ply	mis di rect
mis spell	com prise	mis com pute	mis con duct
mis print	mis teach	re in state	mis cor rect
mis give	mis guide	re ap pear	re con struct
re plant	mis quote	re as sure	re com mence

Words formed by prefixing *per*, *pre*, *post*, *pro* and *inter*.

1	2	1	1
Per vade′	pro pel′	pre en gage′	in ter lace′
per suade	pro tect	pre or dain	in ter leave
pre sume	pre vent	pre dis pose	in ter line
pre clude	pre fix	pre con ceive	in ter vene
post pone	pre tend	pre ma ture	in ter twine
pro vide	per plex	pre sup pose	in ter pose
pro voke	pre judge	pre sur mise	in ter weave
pro duce	pre sent	pre con trive	in ter cede

Words formed by means of other prefixes.

2	1	1
Su per add′	coun ter seal′	out brave′
coun ter check	fore or dain	out grow
coun ter act	su per vene	out face
o ver hang	o ver rate	out sail
o ver match	o ver take	up heave
o ver set	2	up throw
o ver act	sem′i breve	up hold

LESSON 169.

Words spelled alike, but differing in accent and meaning.

Ab'sent, not present.	Ab sent', to keep away.
Ab stract, a summary.	Ab stract, to take away.
Ac cent, a stress of voice.	Ac cent, to mark with accent.
Aug ment, an increase.	Aug ment, to increase.
Au gust, the eighth month.	Au gust, grand.
Col lect, a short prayer.	Col lect, to gather.
Com pact, an agreement.	Com pact, solid.
Com pound, a mixture.	Com pound, to mingle.
Con cert, a musical performance.	Con cert, to contrive.
Con duct, behavior.	Con duct, to guide.
Con fine, a boundary.	Con fine, to restrain.
Con flict, a struggle.	Con flict, to contend.
Con sort, a companion.	Con sort, to associate with.
Con tent, thing contained.	Con tent, satisfied.
Con test, a dispute.	Con test, to dispute.
Con tract, a bargain.	Con tract, to shorten.
Con vert, one who is changed.	Con vert, to change.
Con vict, a guilty person.	Con vict, to prove guilty.
Di gest, a compend.	Di gest, to dissolve in the stomach.
Es cort, a body guard.	Es cort, to accompany.
Es say, an attempt.	Es say, to try.
Ex port, that which is exported.	Ex port, to carry out of a country.
Ex tract, essence drawn out.	Ex tract, to draw out.
Fre quent, happening often.	Fre quent, to visit often.
In sult, an outrage.	In sult, to treat with insolence.
Ob ject, thing acted on	Ob ject, to oppose.
Per fect, complete.	Per fect, to finish.
Pro test, a solemn declaration.	Pro test, to declare solemnly.
Sub ject, one under dominion	Sub ject, to put under.
Sur vey, a view, measure.	Sur vey, to overlook.
Tor ment, pain.	Tor ment, to torture.

LESSON 170.

Words pronounced alike, but spelled differently.

Ail, to trouble.
Ale, malt liquor.
Air, the atmosphere.
Heir, one who inherits.
Ate, did eat.
Eight, a number.
Bail, a surety.
Bale, a bundle of goods.
Bare, naked.
Bear, to carry.
Brake, a thicket.
Break, to force apart.
Fane, a temple.
Fain, gladly.
Feign, to pretend.
Faint, feeble.
Feint, a pretence.
Fair, beautiful.
Fare. food, price of passage.
Gage, a pledge.
Guage, to measure casks.
Gait, manner of walking.
Gate, a kind of door.
Grate, a frame of bars.
Great, large.
Hail, frozen rain.
Hale, strong.
Hair, of the head.
Hare, an animal.
Lade, to load.
Laid, placed.
Stare, to gaze.
Stair, a step.
Stake, a small post.
Steak, a slice of meat.

Lain, participle of *lie*.
Lane, a narrow road.
Made, finished.
Maid, a girl.
Maze, an intricate place.
Maize, Indian corn.
Nay, no.
Neigh, the cry of a horse.
Pail, a vessel for water.
Pale, colorless.
Pane, a square of glass.
Pain, suffering.
Pair, a couple.
Pare, to cut off the outside.
Pear, a kind of fruit.
Plane, a carpenter's tool.
Plain, smooth, manifest.
Pray, to entreat.
Prey, plunder.
Rain, water from the clouds.
Rein, strap of a bridle.
Reign, to rule.
Raise, to lift up.
Raze, to demolish.
Sail, the canvass of a ship.
Sale, act of selling.
Slay, to kill.
Sley, a weaver's reed.
Sleigh, a vehicle on runners.
Vain, fruitless.
Vein, a blood vessel.
Waist, a part of the body.
Waste, to destroy wantonly.
Wait, to tarry.
Weight, heaviness.

LESSON 171.

Words pronounced alike, but spelled differently.

Be, to exist.
Bee, an insect.
Beech, a kind of tree.
Beach, the sea shore.
Beer, malt liquor.
Bier, a carriage for the dead.
Beat, to strike.
Beet, a vegetable.
Dear, beloved, costly.
Deer, an animal.
Feat, an exploit.
Feet, the plural of foot.
Flea, an insect.
Flee, to run away.
Heal, to cure.
Heel, a part of the foot
Hear, to perceive by the ear.
Here, in this place.
Leaf, part of a plant.
Leif, willingly.
Mean, base, low.
Mien, manner.
Meat, animal food.
Meet, to come together.
Mete, to measure.
Need, want.
Knead, to work dough.
Peace, quiet.
Piece, a part.
Peak, top.
Pique, offence.
Die, to expire.
Dye, to color.
Hie, to hasten.
High, lofty, tall.
Peal, a loud sound.
Peel, a skin or rind.
Peer, an equal.
Pier, the support of an arch.
Read, to peruse.
Reed, a plant.
See, to behold.
Sea, the ocean.
Seal, an impression.
Ceil, to make a ceiling.
Seam, a joint.
Seem, to appear.
Seen, beheld.
Scene, a sight.
Seer, a prophet.
Sear, to burn, wither.
Steal, to pilfer.
Steel, carbonized iron.
Team, animals harnessed.
Teem, to abound.
Tear, water of the eye.
Tier, a row.
Week, seven days.
Weak, feeble.
By, near.
Buy, to purchase.
Cite to summon.
Site, a situation.
Sight, a view.
Climb, to ascend.
Clime, climate, region.
Right, proper.
Rite, a ceremony.
Wright, a workman.
Write, to form letters.

LESSON 172.

Words pronounced alike, but spelled differently.

Boar, a male swine
Bore, to make a hole
Boll, a pod
Bowl, a basin
Bow, an instrument for shooting arrows
Beau, a gay gentleman
Coat, an outer garment
Cote, a sheep fold
Coarse, rough
Course, direction
Core, the heart
Corps, a body of troops
Doe, a female deer
Dough, unbaked bread
Fore, in front
Four, twice two
Forth, forward
Fourth, next after the third
Groan, a deep sigh
Grown, increased
Ho, an exclamation
Hoe, a farming tool
Hole, a hollow place
Whole, entire
Hoard, to lay up
Horde, a tribe
Loan, to lend
Lone, solitary
Blue, a color
Blew, did blow
Dew, moisture
Due, owed
Flew, did fly
Flue, a passage for smoke

Lo, behold
Low, humble
Moan, to lament
Mown, cut down
Mote, a small particle
Moat, a ditch
Oar, a pole to row with
Ore, impure metal
Pore, a small tube
Pour, to cause to flow
Pole, a long stick
Poll, the head
Road, a way
Rode, did ride
Rote, a repetition of words
Wrote, did write
Shone, did shine
Shown, exhibited
So, thus
Sow, to scatter
Sew, to work with a needle
Sole, only
Soul, the spirit of man
Sore, an ulcer, painful
Soar, to fly aloft
Throne, seat of a king
Thrown, cast
Toe, part of the foot
Tow, coarse linen
Threw, did throw
Through, from end to end
Hue, color
Hew, to cut
Knew, did know
New, not old

LESSON 173.

Words pronounced alike, but spelled differently.

Bell, an instrument of sound
Belle, a gay young lady
Bred, brought up
Bread, food
Gilt, overlaid with gold
Guilt, crime
Him, that man
Hymn, a sacred song
In, within
Inn, a tavern
Kill, to take away life
Kiln, a sort of stove
Limb, a member
Limn, to paint
Links, connecting rings.
Lynx, an animal
Ring, a circle
Wring, to twist
Not, a negation
Knot, a tie
But, only
Butt, a vessel
Dun, a color
Done, performed
Plum, a kind of fruit
Plumb, a weight attached to a line.
Ruff, a plaited collar
Rough, not smooth
Our, belonging to us
Hour, 60 minutes
Won, did win
One, a number
Ber ry, a small fruit
Bu ry, to cover with earth

Rung, did ring
Wrung, twisted
Sum, the whole
Some, a part
Sun, the source of light
Son, a male child
Ant, an insect
Aunt, a relative
Arc, part of a circle
Ark, a vessel
Hart, an animal
Heart, the seat of life
Herd, a drove
Heard, did hear
Fir, a kind of tree
Fur, soft hair
Cord, a small rope
Chord, a musical harmony
All, the whole
Awl, a pointed tool
Aught, any thing
Ought, bound by duty
Ball, a round body
Bawl, to cry out
Hall, a large room
Haul, to draw
Bow, to bend down
Bough, a branch
Foul, filthy
Fowl, a bird
Les'sen, to make less
Les son, something to be learned
[illegible] y, to collect
[illegible] ee, concourse, a bank

LESSON 174.

Abbreviations used in writing and printing.

A. Answer
A. B. Bachelor of Arts
Acct. Account
A. C. or B. C. Before Christ
A. D. In the year of our Lord
A. M. { Master of Arts / Before noon / In the year of the world }
Att'y. attorney
Bart. Baronet
Bbl. Barrel
B. D. Batchelor of Divinity
Cant. Canticles
Capt. Captain
Cent. or C. A hundred
Chap. Chapter
Chron. Chronicles
Cl. or Clk. Clerk
Co. { Company / County }
Col. { Collector / Colonel / Collossians }
Coll. College
Com. { Commissioner / Commodore }
Con. Contra: on the other hand
Cor. Corinthians
Cr. { Credit / Crediter }
C. S. A. Confedertate States Army.
Cts. Cents
Cwt. A hundred weight

C. S. N. Confederate States Navy
D. D. Doctor of Divinity
Dan. Daniel
Dea. Deacon
Deg. Degree
Dept. Deputy
Deut. Deuteronomy
Do. or Ditto, the same
Dr. { Debtor / Doctor }
E. East
Eccl. Ecclesiastes
Ed. { Editor / Edition }
e. g. For example
Eng. { English / England }
Eph. Ephesians
Esa. Esais
Esq. Esquire
Etc. Et cetera: and so forth
Ex. { Example / Exodus }
Exr. Executor
Ez. Ezra
Fr. { France / Francis }
F. R. S. Fellow of the Royal Society
Gal. Galatians
Gen. { General / Genesis }
Gent. Gentlemen
Geo. George
Gov. Governor

H. B. M. His Brittanic Majesty
Heb. Hebrews
Hhd. Hogshead
Hon. Honorable
H. S. S. Fellow of the Historical Society
Hund. Hundred
Ibid. In the same place
i. e. That is: (id est.)
Id. The same
Inst. Instant
Isa. Isaiah
Jas. James
Jer. Jeremiah
Jno. John
Josh. Joshua
Judg. Judges
Jun. or Jr. Junior
K. King
K. G. Knight of the Garter
K. M. Kingdom
Kt. Knight
Lat. Latitude
Lbs. Pounds
Lev. Leviticus
LL. D. Doctor of Laws
Lieut. Lieutenant
Lon. Longitude
L. S. Place of the Seal
M. Marquis
Maj. Major
Mat. Matthew
Math. Mathematics
M. C. Member of Congress
M. D. Doctor of Medicine
Messrs. { Gentlemen / Sirs
M. P. Member of parliament
Mr. Mister
Mistress
M. S. Manuscript
MSS. Manuscripts
N. North
N. B. Take notice
Neh. Nehemiah
No. number
N. S. New Style
Num. Numbers
Obj. Objection
Obt. Obedient
O. S. Old Style.
P. Page
Pp. Pages
Per. By the; (as, per pard; by the yard)
Per cwt. By the hundred
Pet. Peter
Phil. { Philip / Phillippians
P. M. Post Master. After-noon.
P. O. Post Office
Pres. President
Prof. Professor
Prob. Problem
Prov. Proverbs
P. S. Postscript
Ps. Psalm
Qr. Quarter
Q. { Queen / Question
Rt. Hon. Right Honorable
Rec'd. Received.
Rep. Representatives
Rom. Romans.

Rev. { Revelation / Reverend
S. { Shilling / South
S. A. South America
Sam. Samuel
Sec. { Secretary / Section
Sen. { Senator / Senior.
Sergt. Sergeant
Servt. Servant
St. { Saint / Street
S. T. D. Doctor of Divinity.
S. T. P. Professor of Theology
Thess. Thessalonians
Tho. Thomas
Tim. Timothy
Ult. Ultimo: the last
U. S. A. United States Army
U. S. N. United States Navy
Vide. See
Viz. Namely.
Vs. (Versus.) Against.
W. West.
Wm. William
Yd. Yard
&. And
&c. And so forth.

Abbreviations of the names of places in North America.

Al. Alabama
Ark. Arkansas
Con. or Ct. Connecticut
C. S. Confederate States
C. S. A. Confederate States of America
D. C. District of Columbia
Del. Delaware
Flor. Florida
Geo. or Ga. Georgia
Gua. Guatimala
Ia. Iowa
Ill. Illinois
Ind. Indiana
Ky. Kentucky
L. C. Lower Canada
Lou. or La. Louisiana
Mass. Massachusetts
Md. Maryland
Me. Maine
Mex. Mexico
Mich. Michigan
Miss. Mississippi
Mo. Missouri
N. A. North America
N. B. New Brunswick
N. C. North Carolina
N. H. New Hampshire
N. J. New Jersey
N. S. Novia Scotia
N. Y. New York
O. Ohio
Or. Oregon
Penn. or Pa. Pennsylvania
R. I. Rhode Island
S. C. South Carolina
Tenn. Tennessee
Tex. Texas
U. C. Upper Canada
U. S. United States

U. S. A. United States of America
Vir. or Va. Virginia
Vt. Vermont
Wis. Wisconsin
W. I. West Indies.

Abbreviations for the months, and the days of the week

Jan. January
Feb. February
Mar. March
Ap. or Apr. April
Aug. August
Sept. September
Oct. October
Nov. November
Dec. December
Sun. Sunday
Mon. Monday
Tues. Tuesday
Wed. Wednesday
Thurs. Thursday
Fri. Friday
Sat. Saturday

LESSON 175.

Names of Rivers in the Confederate States.

Alabama
Altamaha
Apalachicola
Appomattox
Arkansas
Black Warrior
Black Water
Broad
Big Black
Brazos
Colorado
Cape Fear
Catawba
Chattahoochee
Chectowatchie
Combahee
Chowan
Coosa
Clinch
Cow Pasture
Cumberland
Dan
Deep
Edisto
Escambia
Flint
French Broad
Great Pedee
Haw
Holston
Jackson
James
Kanawha
Little Missouri
Little Pedee
Little Red
Mermentau
Mississippi
Mobile
Neuse
Ocmulgee
Oconee
Ogeechee
Oscilla
Pascagoula
Pearl
Perdido
Potomac
Rappahannock
Red
Roanoke
Sabine
Saluda
Santee
Saltillo
Savannah
St. Francis
St. John's
St. Mary's
Shenandoah
Staunton
Suwanee
Tallapoosa
Tar
Tombigbee
Tallahatchee
Trinity
Tennessee
White
Yazoo

Milton Keynes UK
Ingram Content Group UK Ltd.
UKHW020056080824
1193UKWH00011B/178

9 781014 964779